MW00647649

Julian teaches

SELF-DISCOVERY & MANIFESTATION

through June K. Burke

★

BURKE-SROUR PUBLICATIONS
La Grangeville, New York

Copyright 1988 June K. Burke
ISBN: 0-929377-00-1
Library of Congress Number: 88-071423

ALL RIGHTS RESERVED. NO PART OF THIS BOOK MAY BE
REPRODUCED OR UTILIZED IN ANY FORM OR BY ANY MEANS,
ELECTRONIC OR MECHANICAL INCLUDING PHOTO COPYING,
RECORDING, OR BY ANY INFORMATION STORAGE OR RETRIEVAL
SYSTEM; WITHOUT PRIOR WRITTEN PERMISSION OF THE
PUBLISHER.

Burke-Srour Publications Inc.
Route 3, Box 133
La Grangeville, NY 12540

First Edition: 1989
Printed and bound in the United States of America
Cover and Interior Design: Phillip Eric Sobel

DEDICATION

This book is dedicated with love and gratitude to Miriam L. Chandler without whom nothing written would have begun.

Thanks, Mir—for all the hand-holding, prodding, and laughter along the way.

June

★

PREFACE

The book you are about to read first came into being as a series of lectures presented in New York City. When the lectures were presented, the impact they had on those participating was so strong and so positive, we realized we had to make them available to everyone who wanted and needed them. Although tapes of the classes were available, many people expressed a preference for a visual study guide; so the long haul of transcribing, editing, and writing began. Busy time schedules slowed the process and bogged us down at times, but we persevered. The effort has brought forth this first book of Julian's teachings and created the work process which will permit his other books to come forth more readily.

ACKNOWLEDGMENTS

This book did not come into being overnight. Before any written attempt was made, there were months of discussion, questions, sighs, laughter and love. The manuscript itself became a multi-parent child. We also were blessed with the magnificent spiritual energy of Julian guiding us along the way.

When channeling, I am in a total state of amnesia. This calls for a strong support system when teaching publicly. I have been blessed with just such a system of caring people throughout my twenty-six years of work. My husband, Bill, has been my right hand in all my efforts. His love and support on all levels has made the path brighter and easier.

A very special *thank you* goes to our children Janet, Ellen, and Bill for accepting a different kind of mother and for giving so much of their time to others in need. Special hugs to our granddaughter Kari Ellen for the joy she brings into our lives.

I wish to acknowledge, too, the extended spiritual family who are so dear and who have always been there. To Joy and Saul Srour, Renate and Behram Dhunjishaw, Leela and Barry Burkan, Dorthy and Frank De Sotto, Judith Lackamp, and George Ruby go my gratitude and love for their constant support.

To Lela Traver, a very special *thank you* for all the years of shared growth and love. Thanks go to Nicholas Theo for copy reading and to Mark Love for his hours of work with Daniel Kitchen on the computer. To the many who offered their support, my thanks and love. The dedication of this book to Miriam L. Chandler only briefly touches what she has meant to this project. To each and every one of you goes my heart-felt thanks for sharing in the joy of self-discovery and the manifestation of this book.

J. K. B.

EDITOR'S COMMENTS

Working with the Julian material has been both a powerful and transforming experience. I first encountered Julian at a public lecture he gave some years ago. Since that time I have had the privilege of working with him which has led to an opportunity to assist in preparing his material for publication.

It is an understatement to say that the keys Julian has given in *Self-Discovery and Manifestation* are anything less than transforming. The final proof of the validity of any metaphysical teaching is in its direct applicability to the mundane events of everyday life. To this I must add that from my experience, this material has been a major factor in my personal evolution and transformation.

If the reader will allow himself to view his life from the perspective that Julian gives, I believe he will experience extraordinary results. It is a practical and easy method which permits one to understand one's self.

We are now in the Aquarian Age, the age of the circle, when lost and hidden knowledge is going to again be brought forth. This material comes to us from a dimension that we little understand or know. It is refreshing to receive assistance from a source that I have found to be remarkably free of criticism and absolutely free of judgment. This quality is of itself a perspective rarely experienced on this earthly plane. Words are utterly inadequate in describing the ecstasy that comes from working with a force so open and accepting, yet a force so totally devoted to the service and assistance of mankind. Therein lies an understanding from which we could all learn.

Daniel W. Kitchen

HOW JUNE AND JULIAN BEGAN

My association with Julian took a long time to build. It was forming even before I was totally aware of his presence. As a child, I was psychic. I knew who was on the telephone before it was answered. I knew when packages were going to arrive before the mail was delivered. I thought everybody did. Somewhere along the way, probably because of peer pressure, I ceased to use my ability. It was not intentional. It just happened. Some twenty-six years later, I would again remember the gift.

It was when my third child was born, that my awareness was put in motion again. Six hours after delivering a beautiful son, I had a postpartum hemorrhage. Veins collapsed and I had the death experience. How does one describe dying? I would have to describe it as the most beautiful experience I have had in this lifetime. I experienced the tunneling into light and witnessed color spectrums beyond those we understand. Take our known color spectrum and amplify it one hundred-fold and you might come close. We just do not have the magnificent kaleidoscope I witnessed there. The most beautiful part of the experience was that I was separate from nothing. I was one with everything in existence. I became aware of the white light and a voice. When asked if I wished to fulfill my destiny, I agreed. I had not the faintest idea what that meant at the time. What could it possibly mean but the chance to raise my son? Once I agreed to the destiny, I was turned around, no longer able to look into that world. Now I found myself looking down into the hospital room, watching the two teams of doctors and nurses working on me. I knew it was me but felt no emotional attachment at all. As I watched I became aware of the compassion on the faces of those working on me. Immediately, the thought came that I had to go back and tell them it was okay, that I did not hurt anymore. With the thought, came the return to the body, surgery and recovery. Now the search began.

God had always been a presence in my life, but now I wanted a more intimate realization of the God within. I wanted to know more about the world I had seen. I remembered that psychic side of myself and wished to understand it more fully. The quest began. The path led to meditation, and the meditation to the development of the deep trance work. During meditation I was prepared physically and emotionally for a safe and smooth merger of the energies that would permit us to work as a team.

J. K. B.

JULIAN'S STATEMENT

I am a seraph of the order of seraphim, that which you would call "angelic force." From the beginning of time, I have been a bridge between two worlds. I have never been in a physical body other than borrowed ones. In our varying energy patterns, angelic forces are given assignments which they carry forth in the universe. My assignment has been to be a teacher of truth, a deliverer of God's messages, and a deliverer of mankind through his own potential. Thus, from the beginning of time, I have been a bridge between the unseen world and the seen. I have watched cultures be born, come to fruition, and die. It is my job to try to know and understand the culture, and the vernacular of that culture, in order to help man to better his potential.

The angelic forces of the universe were created to be the friends and guardians of mankind and all creation. We have no desire other than to assist. Our fulfillment is in observing mankind's growth and transition into higher planes. Each angelic force has its own particular assignment. Some deal with the plant and nature world, others with the animal kingdom. There is no thing of God's creation in the earth that does not have a guardian force that is overseeing its advancement within its own species. It is meant to be that all things evolve.

Through the book you are about to read, I will lead you toward a greater realization of your own actions. Understanding your thought patterns and inner fears will permit you to learn to release, grow, and find fulfillment. It will be my joy to be that guide.

I have asked that the book be left as it was given, as a teaching form. Thus, as you read you will feel that I am talking to *you* and that will be as it is meant to be.

So be it !
Julian

SPECIAL NOTE

Julian has a way of mixing his pronouns with absolute disregard for singular and plural; masculine and feminine; and first, second, and third person. The end result is a strong paragraph, the meaning of which is perfectly clear. Since this is typically his way of speaking, we have chosen to leave his pronouns as they are.

The use of the word "man" in these teachings refers to mankind, versus the animal or mineral kingdoms. It has no reference to gender.

There have been times when we thought Julian was making up words only to discover they are archaic forms from which our words are derived. In those instances we have left the word as he has used it. If unclear, we have placed the current use in parentheses.

We have bowed to a seraphim's mode.

★

CONTENTS

**Love is based on trust,
and trust on acceptance.
To love is to accept!**

—Julian

SELF-DISCOVERY

CHAPTER ★ I

The Meaning of Self-Discovery

Self-discovery does not mean the contemplation of the navel, the shutting-out of the world, or tearing apart of the self. It is the acceptance of where you are with a fuller understanding of that space and how you got there. Whether you want to change it or not depends on your own free will.

It is very important that each person bring to themselves the understanding of who they are, what they are, and why they are. Hopefully, this will help you work through many emotional traumas and will help you work through many individual conflicts. Each and every one of you, no matter how spiritually evolved you feel you are, has within you certain parts of yourself that war with other parts of yourself. By learning to modify those parts, you are able to bring perfect harmony, which permits perfect vision and perfect realization. The purpose, then, will be for you to listen and understand as you break some of the molds that have trapped you for many years.

I would like you to be willing to look openly at yourself and learn about yourself. Be able to say, "I've got a terrible temper," and be willing to learn from the recognition of that facet of yourself. Through this, you will come to the realization of who you really are without anxiety.

It is important for you to realize that you are a triad. You are mind, body, and spirit. Only when each of these is functioning in equal balance are you truly yourself. What does spirit mean? Does it mean dogmatic practice? If a dogmatic practice is the means to God which helps you to symbolize and practice it, yes. If it does not, no. Each man finds God in his own way. The first place to look for Him is in the one place that no one ever looks: within yourself, for that is where He dwells. He is not a dictator. He gave you one gift which He will not rescind and that is free will. By that free will, you make decisions. Some decisions may appear to be wrong decisions at the time. In reality, each decision teaches you something and helps you to grow and to know. Therefore, they are all good decisions.

As we progress we are going to take the mind, body, and soul of you and integrate it, so that you are able to communicate with yourself without a sense of discord.

You are a triad and each part of yourself has an equal importance. Each part of your being, physical, mental, and inner self or spirit, the God-self, must be in touch with each other part. There are several ways to do this. Meditation. Prayer. Dream state. Prayer is when you talk to God, and meditation is when you are listening to God. In the dream state, you open yourself to the universal consciousness so that you can be taught. All of these phases are important to the harmonic of the self.

It is important to meditate daily on yourself. Enter that meditation openly. See it as a time of interaction with *all* of *you*. Question the irritants of life. Let the answers come from within yourself. Do not be surprised if they tell you something you do not want to hear.

If the answer is one you do not particularly want, you are bound to get emotional about it. You get emotional as a first reaction. Then you take that energy and use it productively to straighten out the situation. Do not wallow in the emotion.

Meditation is a tool; it is the key to all awareness! The object of the blissful quiet is to relax the senses enough to move beyond the physical senses into the higher sensorium. The spirit senses are able to cross all barriers and give you information, knowledge, or the feeling that is right for you.

If anyone meditates forty-five minutes, they have meditated quite enough. If they meditate an hour, they have gone a little too far. If they go beyond that, forget it; because they are taking themselves into a space and leaving themselves there. Anything that is going to happen to you is going to happen in the first forty-five minutes. After that, you are using it as an escape route. It can become detrimental if it is permitting you to escape life and not face life and deal with it. What you are supposed to do is get from it the tools you need, the comprehension and the understanding, and bring them back into the life so that the life can move forward.

You should recognize that there are different forms of meditation and that there are times when you meditate and you do not know you are meditating. Many people meditate while they are driving. If you understand that meditation is an altered state of consciousness, you are able to understand that the conscious mind is so busy doing all the things that it is supposed to do that the mind's other two parts, the subconscious and the super-conscious, are free to communicate. The super-conscious mind is the mind of the spirit body, the mind that directs you by your intuition. The subconscious rules the body through the pituitary gland. They commune. If the super-conscious can get something to the subconscious without the personality's conscious mind intervening, there is a chance that this information will be released to you later. The result is a lesson either during the dream state or at a quiet time. This is very often what happens when you suddenly *know* something. All of a sudden you know, and you are no longer confused about an issue that has been bothering you. The answer many not be the answer you hoped for, or the answer you really thought it would be, but it is the answer and you know it. From that point on, you can handle it and can act on it.

One of the things that I have observed most in your world is that the one person whom nobody wants to be alone with is themselves. Have you ever noticed? You put the radio on, you put the television on, you put the stereo on, anything to have a little noise around because if you are alone with you, you might have to talk to you. You are going to learn to talk to you and to recognize the beauty and totality of you.

The first thing you must realize is that there is a part of you that is going to fight the realization of the reality of you. The personality-self, the ego-ruled self, says, "Do not listen," but once you get that personality self listening, it can become part of the reality self. It does not mean you are going to go around like zombies, not being able to have a personality, have fun, or joke. All of that is living and that is all right. Please, if you must discard something, do not discard your sense of humor, for without it, man is very dull. The ability to laugh *at yourself and* with *others* is one of the greatest gifts you have, and it is the saving feature of many disagreements. To suddenly be able to laugh about it makes it all right. As you work through, you are going to take the self, all three parts of you, and integrate them so that you are able to communicate with yourself without any sense of discord.

The foundation of most discord is inflexibility. The emotional attitude of a fixed realization says, "This is it." This is the only way you have ever known it, and you do not want it any other way. You can get terribly caught up in your own little cocoon. The lesson here is to let go and to be willing to be flexible. Most people confuse being flexible with being dictated to. Do not confuse the two issues. Flexibility means that having examined all things, one has found another route or way which leads to a better method to the goal in sight. That is flexibility. Flexibility comes from being willing to see the full spectrum of what can be. It does not mean always being the underdog. It means being humble, and realize humbleness does not mean subservience. People think to be humble is to be less. No, to be humble is to accept that it is all right for things not to be all right and then to do something about it. Humbleness is acceptance. If you accept a situation, you are able to overcome it. It means you are willing to work *with* the situation and work your way out of it. You will notice I said "with" the situation, not against it. When you use your energy to fight the situation, you can never understand it; and you can never find your way out of it. It is important for you to realize that *how* you use your energy will make the difference.

Flexibility and acceptance are two key words in bringing change into the life. To become less inflexible permits you to better understand and cope with outward influences which we will call "atmospheric conditions."

In any gathering, the persons on your left and your right are creating an atmospheric condition for you. The one behind you and the one in front of you are also creating an atmospheric condition. Thus, those four energies surrounding you are touching your energy and causing a condition for you to work within. Have you ever noticed that when you meet somebody and after talking to them, you immediately have your back up? You meet somebody else and talk to them and immediately they are all right. It could be your inflexibility that does not let you stand the first one, or it could be that the energies are repelling each other. Each of you has an energy that exudes from you, and just as some magnets attract and some repel, so do some energies. It does not mean that this cannot be overcome; it only means that the initial response is, "Stay away! I am not too sure I want to let this energy into my space." It is then something you work through and, by working through it, come to understand.

It is important to recognize that while these words may seem very clear (you take step A and then step B, et cetera), when you are dealing with emotional energies, it is not that clear. You have a feeling and you would like to do something about it, but what? One moment you say, "I could do this, or I could do that." The next question is, "Why should I? Why should I stick my neck out? Why should I become vulnerable? I will stay here in my safe little spot and wait for the other fellow to make a move." In the meantime, the other fellow sitting in his little cocoon is saying, "Why should I? Why should I stick my neck out? Why should I make myself vulnerable?" If you are going to interact with the whole self or another, the first thing you have to do is be willing to take a chance, be willing to reach out, and be willing to be vulnerable. Being vulnerable, believe it or not, can be a lot of fun. It does not always have to be bad. Remember, the only thing that can change the space you are in is *you*. You can get up and leave it, you can start thinking thoughts that can change it, or you can make believe it is not happening at all. How you choose to think is a matter of *your* free will. Remember, by *you* changing the way that you think about the person next to you, you will affect how they feel toward you. This means you are changing the atmosphere of the person next to you. Soon the whole room will become a changed atmosphere.

You exude energy. It is that energy which changes the atmosphere around you. The only way the atmosphere around you can be changed is within *you*. If you do not take the first step in you, it can never happen in the atmosphere around you. Remember, that as you change your thought pattern and your energy, you are influencing the energy of the person next to you. At that point they are influencing the people around them and soon you have a room full of changed energies. It is important for you to realize the power *within you* to change you, which in turn changes that which is around you. There can be no more important thing for you to understand than the God-given ability to create change from within the self.

Sometimes when you think there is no place else to go with something you are trying to accomplish, you must realize the time has come for a change in how you approach the situation. Very often man tries so hard he blocks his ability to make the necessary changes within. If you cannot make something happen, perhaps it is time to step away from it for a moment. Try doing something else. Succeeding at something else brings back the inner feeling of the ability to accomplish and the fulfillment from that accomplishment.

You can then go back to the original situation and better see the alterations in thinking that are necessary to make it succeed. When you have done this, two things have occurred: you have been flexible enough to find a new route to the thing you were trying to do, and you have learned that by stepping away and accomplishing in some other way, you reinforced the realization of your ability to accomplish.

You have in your world the statement that it is better to light one candle in the darkness than to curse the darkness. It is better to have one positive thought in a room of gloom than to add to the gloom. You must bring the point of where you *want* to be to the point of where you *are*. You cannot change your feelings by thinking the same thoughts that go with the feelings. If you are thinking *rainy day* and your association with a rainy day is gloomy, dull, and terrible, you are going to begin to think gloomy, dull and terrible thoughts until you and everyone that comes into your presence are totally down and miserable for the day. If, perchance, you start thinking instead about the sun when it was shining, the sunny hill, the pines in the sunshine, or any other happy thought or experience you have had, you will begin to find that even though the rain might still be intense, you are not feeling gloomy. You would have changed the thought pattern and what was emanating from you. You would have brought brightness into it, and that is contagious. Once you start that, others are going to pick it up, and it is going to move, and it is going to work.

Sometimes when you think there is no place else to go, try changing your thought pattern. When you are trying to make something happen and it will not happen, try making *something else* happen. By making something else happen, you put into motion the energy of *something* happening. You feel a sense of accomplishment and fulfillment because something worked. Then you can go back to the first thing that was not working, and chances are, you will make it work. You will have accepted that there was something else your energy could do.

Most of the inner grief that one experiences deals with not recognizing that the moment something has happened, it has already become the past. Once upon a time, when I started this chapter—you see? The next word is now, but by the time I go to the third one after that, it is the past. When something happens to you, you must stop bringing it back by thought patterns and actions that keep it alive and suffering in front of you. "I am this way because Father yelled at me when I was five." "I had an argument with my girlfriend." "Back in the twentieth millennium I collided with another star." You are this way because you have chosen to be this way. You are choosing to let the atmosphere around you become you. Instead, be willing to use your own positive energy to change the atmosphere around you. You cannot always become the other person's anger or the incident that hurt you when you were five. After all, if a cookie is denied to a five-year old, it is a painful thing; but if I were to deny you a cookie today, could you really consider it as painful? You must look at each incident in your life through the understanding of the moment. You must permit the harmonic of mind, body, and soul to rule your thought patterns and your actions.

As I have said many times before, the thought is the conception, the spoken word is the birth, and the action is the rearing of the child. You are going to think it, say it, and you are also going to have to do something about it if it is going to become anything. People keep saying, "Someday I'd like to . . ." They start that when they are twelve, and when they are eighty-two, they are still saying, "I'd like to." With luck, they still have time. The thing you must realize is that you must put into action some part of that dream today. Do not try to make the whole dream in one instant, but take a segment of it that can be a reality and work with that. "I want to dance. I want to be recognized." You can dream forever or you can start taking dance lessons. All the aching muscles and the sweat feed the dream by action. The moment you start to do that, the dream takes shape and form. You have not only thought it, but you have begun to act upon it.

Sometimes you have to role-play in order to convince yourself that it can be so. In your world, I have looked many times and seen very humble abodes. Yet, a cheerfulness would be there because of the energies put out in love by those who were in that abode. In some small way, brightness and beauty would have been brought to that home. I have seen others who have plenty sit and not enjoy one thing that they have because they did not have some other thing. If you do not take time to enjoy what you have, there is no way that you can bring joy by adding something else to it. A person who thinks he will finally be happy when he takes the new trip, or will finally be happy when somebody dies and leaves him money, is totally in error. I can see the thoughts. The one thing to remember is that, in those thought patterns, you are locking yourselves into less.

You have got to be able to work with what you have. What is expected of you at any time is to do the best you can with what you have—no more. That works two ways. You can say, "All right, I may be riding a motor scooter right now, but a car will come my way in time. I'll take good care of the motor scooter; I'll bless it and love it, and let *it* work for me," or you can say, "Well, I cannot afford to have the silver and the sterling that I might like, but stainless steel looks very nice." Good! Enjoy it! If you are giving the setting its due, you will have as beautiful a table, as lovingly received and as greatly enjoyed as the finest silver that could ever be. If your concern is for the silver, it may not be for your guests. Use where you *are* and make *it* a space that is good, and from that, let it grow. Recognize also that what we are speaking of happens at all levels of life and this has nothing to do with monetary return. As I said before, many who have everything feel poor, and some who have much less feel rich.

All that we have been talking about is leading to the realization that within you is the key to your release from preconceived ideas of what happiness is.

Happiness is not the house, the car, the coat, or whatever. Happiness is being in the space you are in at any point in time and thoroughly permitting yourself to be one with what is going on. You have the statement in your world that says, "Take time to smell the flowers." It is true. You are in a world of escalated energies and all of you have the feeling of what you call the "rat race." Take time to be. It is most important. There is another statement in your world that I like very much. It says something like, "Grow where you are planted." And that is true. The essence is the same. Where you are is where you begin to make it happen. While you dream of other vistas, merge that with the reality of where you are and work from there. Then, and only then, can you truly change your world. Do not fight it, join it. Permit yourself to stop being angry because you find yourself in the spot you are in. That anger is where the misery comes from. You get so angry at finding yourself in a situation you do not want to be in that you expend great energy on anger. Instead, begin to work toward what you need to have, a change in thinking patterns to break old molds and break preconceived conceptions. A lot of things are very different from even ten, fifteen, or twenty years ago. You work with the understanding that you change by acceptance and you build what you want out of it.

If things are not as you like them, accept that it is all right for things not to be all right. Do not say, "This misery is going to be mine. It is going to be part of me." Instead, work at being the point of light in that so-called dark situation. Remember that how a situation is judged—good or bad—is very often based on the viewpoint. Remember that child with the cookie? The fact that he can have it after supper does not make any difference; he wants it now. In your world, timing is most important. There is truly a time for all things; and if you permit timing to flow as it is supposed to, making use of every step along the way toward your goal, you will come out all right.

Let me give you an example. Many years ago, a man was a man when he was eleven or twelve. He took on the full responsibility of a job. When he was fifteen, he was considered old enough to do his own thing, go his own way. He had already been working for three or four years. Females in that time were considered adults at very young ages. They were marrying at twelve, thirteen, and fourteen. Now cultural changes have come, and you find that maturity is supposed to be at the age of twenty-one. The society says that at twenty years, eleven months, and thirty days you become a man. What have you done before that to become a man? There was a time when a little girl was a little girl. Today you have all sorts of things such as training bras and pre-training bras. This little girl at the age of ten or eleven is not the adult she was in earlier times, but instead, a sophisticated child who now thinks that she can handle the world. This creates all kinds of chaos for the self. But why? Because time has escalated. Time is pushing her into sophistication without the maturity factor to go with it.

I must repeat it would seem that self-esteem in your world today is based on what you wear on your derriere. If you do not have a name across the derriere, you are not "in," you are not acceptable. It is the culture and the time. Man has placed the responsibility for how he feels about himself *outside* himself. The eleven- or twelve-year-olds of years ago had already felt the self-esteem of establishing themselves as persons. When things happened in the life, they still relied on the fact that they did whatever they did well. It was not, in that period, based on exterior things. Stop putting your value on things outside yourself. You are a divine child of God with divine rights of your own and you shall be fulfilled.

He who lives in his head has little room to grow.

————————————Julian

The divine right
of discernment
says:
you may like or dislike
something, and relates to
the ego-personality.

The divine law of love
says:
"Love—unconditionally,"
and relates to the soul.

—————————————————————Julian

CHAPTER ★ II

The Seven-Year Cycles

When one is coming to grips with parts of one's self from within the self, you may at times feel a bit ill at ease. Some of the statements that I make may seem to you to be a little strange, or perhaps, do not seem to relate to you. When you are dealing with identity, you are dealing with sensing factors of the personality. I touched upon them a little in the previous chapter, and we are going to touch upon them further.

You enter the world as an energy, totally aware, totally open and totally knowledgeable. Everything you need to achieve the goals in your life is given to you. During the course of your life, you are gradually influenced by others. Perhaps, in your early years, you can say that the sins of the father are delivered upon the child. What does that mean? It means that the prejudices and the opinions of the parent are visited upon the child, and if a child hears it long enough, he is going to accept it as fact. What other images do children have to turn to early in their lives but those that are governing or raising them? Every one of you has been in that position. You have all been that wee babe.

You go through rounds of seven. For the first seven years, you are pliable and pretty much accept that what is said is so. At the age of seven, there comes a growing awareness that you must assert your inner self. What happens? At about the age of five, there begins an aggressiveness, an aggressiveness that says, "No!" By the age of seven, you have begun to put a rationale with the aggressiveness—"No, because . . ." It is really something very magical that is talking. It is the inner self saying that you are a being who must hold on to your identity. Although you are pliable, you must not permit yourself to be shaped and molded to that which you, in reality, are not.

It may seem to you farfetched that a seven-year-old is thinking in these terms. They are not consciously thinking this way, but they are thinking subconsciously, in the reality of themselves. They are feeling the demand to hold on to that identity with which they were born.

The seven-year cycles are a flow, a rhythm. It is not something cut and dried. You may feel it coming or going two years in advance or two years later as it builds, peaks, and wanes.

The seven-year cycles are an evolutionary spiral. They belong to every being that has ever been created. There is no one who does not go through them. Every seven years there is, within the system, a total change. It is a soul's demand to be seen as an individual, not as a collective. At the age of seven, the first realization of self begins to occur. The restlessness that is felt within is due to body chemistry changes from that of an infant to that of a child. The seven-year-old stands firm in his belief in himself. It is then that an aggressiveness seems to occur, and the child of seven gives that defiant, "No."

At the age of fourteen comes the second series of defiances. Once again a total change of the system occurs. It is a creation of a private space and the physical preparation for adulthood. It is here that voice change occurs within the male, and the female body development begins. You will hear everybody in your world talking about teenagers. They talk about them as if they were lepers. They are not! They are trying to find their identities, but now a new ingredient has been added. They are not only being shaped and molded by that in which they live, the family unit, but also by that which they occupy and encounter outside of that family unit—schools, playgrounds, grocery stores, every place a child goes. Because there are many of them who are "in the same boat," they will group together.

Did you ever hear the magical "they?" "They" are all doing it. "They" say it is okay. The parent also has that mythical "they." The parents constantly refer to the government as "they." The magical, mythical "they" has already become the one to blame it all on.

If there has been a feeling of subjugation or denial emotionally, the energy of this cycle may be directed at that source. This often brings clarification to feelings.

The point I want to make is that at each seven-year round, there is an aggressiveness equal to the level of physical energy released. That aggressiveness, if treated with respect and guided, can become a very powerful tool in the life of the individual. If, on the other hand, it is treated as a case of leprosy, if the individuals are shoved aside and not listened to, then there is going to be a buildup of that energy *added to the next seven-year cycle.*

In order to be free, to be separate, and to begin to break away from energies that have confined them, the fourteen-year-old will build a nemesis. They build an ogre. Whether it is father, mother, or grandmother, somebody becomes the one that is just too terrible in the whole world and makes them have to use their aggressiveness. It is so delightfully normal, even though it may be a bit of an irritant in the physical world. Everyone of you has gone through the rounds. They are universal. This helps the fourteen-year-old to protect itself from invasion, an invasion on all levels—mentally, emotionally, and spiritually. He will back away and say, "Give me space."

After fourteen, the next time that most people become aggressive is at twenty-one. It is now time for them to definitely cut ties and move to be on their own. At twenty-one the cycle changes. The attitude is, "Don't tell me, I know it." This is preparation emotionally and mentally for adulthood.

The greatest realization of adulthood occurs at twenty-eight! The cycles of seven, fourteen, and twenty-one all deal with internal changes, and the cycle of twenty-eight is the first step in external integration with the rest of the world. Very often the thought is, "Okay, world, what have you got to give me?" At that time you are experiencing your first Saturn return, and here the person begins to reach outward from the self. You enter your Saturn return every twenty-eight-and-a-half years. It is a cycle. We are not talking about astrology when we talk about this. Saturn deals with teaching and relationships to time, even though it is timeless. It deals with time in cycles of unfoldment. There seems to be a pressure, an irritation when that return comes around in relation to your energies. It does not come to "get you." It comes and presents you with an opportunity. The energy of a Saturn return lets you do something else with yourself if you desire to. It is a marvelous energy.

At thirty you are still moving out of the Saturn return, so there should be an impetus to great change in the self. You should have a desire to do new things and to head in new directions. The thirty-fifth year is the cutting of the emotional umbilical cord and true emotional adulthood arrives. Here one stands alone, unable to be influenced by the emotional attitudes of others. It is the opportunity to become free of emotional stigma of the past and is a major change position in the seven-year cycles. At thirty-five comes a solidity factor that gives you the opportunity to say, "Wait a minute. If I am going to do that, whom do I have to listen to?" If you are cutting and severing the influences of the past, you are probably, for the first time, deciding for yourself what you want to do. It is a freedom factor. Understand when we talk about the cycles of growth, we are not saying that at the age of thirty-five you cut off everybody you know and hate your parents. We are saying you finally separate those concepts which are really yours from those which belong to somebody else.

At thirty-five, there is a solidification and a disassociation with all that was before. At this time there is the potential for true identity release. One finds himself most apt to be a new individual, ready to roll with new decisions, most of them created by the self. There is usually at this time a major force that functions within the life system which permits you to finally really, truly, stand alone. That may sound as if it is a terribly long wait, but please understand that you are supposed to be enjoying the road along the way. Every age, every seven-year aggression, and every seven-year unfoldment has special things to be known, understood, and worked with. There is no time in your life that does not have validity.

In each seven-year cycle there is a complete body chemistry change and a need for unfoldment, a release from preconceived attitudes. This gives a freedom which permits major change in attitudes, in relationships, and in career.

The forty-second year is a major change because it is the polarity of the twenty-eighth year. Here, the integration of the whole self occurs. The view is not, "World, what can you give me?" as in the twenty-eighth year, but, "World what have I got to give you?" It is the realization of all the growth that has occurred and the ability to use it in its most productive way. At forty-two you may begin to have doubts about your life. These doubts are not negative. They are based on the growth gained in the interim years between thirty-five and forty-two. This creates an ability to question whether you wish to maintain your life as it is or whether new changes are imminent. Doubt can be very positive if it is leading you to be suspect of something in your life that is not good for you.

After forty-two comes forty-nine. Forty-nine continues to be a doubting period, and sometimes it can become more negative. At forty-nine, there are rumblings of, "Where am I headed, what do I do, and do I want this." There is this funny feeling that maybe it is too late. It is *never* too late. There can be the sense of "Where have I been and what have I done with my life?" If this feeling is permitted to join the ego, there is usually a tremendous thrust outward to prove that you are still in the first five seven-year cycles.

At forty-nine, one begins to question what they have in their life and very often discovers that they can let go of something in their life in order to have room to take on something new. There is a tendency to view this cycle as the last chance to be productive or to show their ability and to make a name for themselves. Part of the reason for this is that the next seven-year cycle also ties in again to a Saturn return. The forty-ninth year gives you the opportunity to approach letting go in small ways, so that you are more prepared for that wonderful time that the seven-year cycle of fifty-six will bring you.

At fifty-six, there is a very often a tendency in your world to let go of everything that has been and to take on a whole new life style. At forty-nine you are still trying to say, "I got to make it before I have to let go."

Realize that the first seven cycles from seven to forty-nine are the spiraling of all change *within you*. Those that come after that time are the expansion of the same seven spirals once again. The seven-year cycles are normal productive parts of man's evolutionary process. In these writings, we will investigate them and see how they touch you personally, how you can use each of the seven-year cycles to break away from that which is no longer serving you, and move forward to new horizons and potential.

What I am going to ask you to do is to very openly think about your first seven years. I want you to think of an incident that occurred that you felt emotional about. Whether it be a happy or sad experience does not matter. There will always be some memory of something. Think about your first seven years and think about what you can relate to.

Many people do not remember a childhood experience because they participated in it passively. They enjoyed it, they thought it was fine, but it was a passive and flowing thing. It was not something that had a shock value which anchored that point in time in the life. Some anchors are good and some are bad. There is often a tendency to tie yourself emotionally to something in the past—good or bad—so strongly that you cannot move forward in the present.

I watched a seven-year-old child recently discussing with her mother a book on childbirth. The book showed a beautiful pictorial illustration of a child's birth. The child, very interested, looked at these pictures and said,

"Oh! Look at these. Oh! Look at the little feet, the little hands. What is that?" She was speaking of sperm. Her mother explained to her that this was the seed carried by the father. A little further on she said, "Whoops, I don't think I'm ready for that page, mother! Let's skip that page." She did not really know what that page was. Something in her said her seven-year-old comprehension at that time was not ready for that page. There is magnificent wisdom within a child at that early age. When you listen to it as openly and willingly as most seven-year-olds do, you can know when it is enough. She did not feel cheated by not looking at that page. Something told her she was not ready for that. Something told her to go back and look at the little hands and little feet. This seven-year-old girl in truth explored the inner reality of birth and understood it as a beautiful, living, wonderful thing— a miracle. I brought that example to you because it was such a wonderful visualization of seven-year-old wisdom, which at times is more like seventy-year-old wisdom.

Each energy cycle is one of movement in relationship to man's cycles of growth. Man has been given everything he needs to make all the changes he wants to make in himself and his life, provided he listens to the reality of the inner self and is not guided solely by the external self. The external guidance will have to do with the ego. Ego permits you to move forward. Without it, you might become too passive, but your inner reality guides you from your highest space.

Cycle reactions will vary according to the responsibility load of the time. Some people at forty-nine may still be seriously involved in raising their children. They don't feel free to let go and take on something new. They can use the next cycle of fifty-six to accomplish this as long as they don't take the attitude that it is too late. The perspective on how to do it may have changed, but the ability to accomplish has not. The point is that there is a natural release of energy every seven years which encourages you to move forward and make changes. It helps to keep you from getting stuck in a rut. Flow with these cycles and you will find change less fearful.

The beat of your heart is the heartbeat of the universe.
———————————————————————————————Julian

**True friendship is
as the dawn and sunset:
always there,
always changing,
and always joy!**
—————————————————Julian

CHAPTER ★ III

Self-Development

Self-discovery leads to a better emotional comprehension of the self which puts less pressure on the individual and, therefore, sometimes helps to avoid emotional problems.

In understanding yourself and coming to better know yourself, you are going to face feelings deep within. Do not be afraid to cry while you are working with those feelings. Realize that tears are a purging. The emotion hits you, the tears well up and come out. That is a purging and that is okay. Once the tears have released the pressure, go back to the incident that occurred. Take the hurt out of that space and time and bring it forward to the present. Take a good look at it and re-evaluate its importance *now*. You may find it has no real value and is not worth holding on to. Go back and take it out of its root place so you can get a good view of it. Very often something that happened in younger years becomes an emotional problem because of a sense of guilt. Somewhere in there you know you caused part of it, but if it is way out of focus, what good can it be to you today?

As you develop you will find it easier to understand why you are in a given situation. As you understand that situation better, it is easier to let go. The thing you have to realize is that when you begin to expend too much time on a problem, you are feeding it. If you are spending time on it and you are not getting anywhere with it, then you have to back away from it and let it go. Let it fall into its proper perspective; otherwise, you are building a kitten into a tiger.

If you have had a heated and emotional exchange, very often you will feel like a fool the next day. If you can accept that you acted like a fool and if you can see it as ridiculous, you can alter the vibration of that emotional exchange. Always be willing to look at *your* true participation in the incident, realizing that sometimes you will not like what you see. Either way, you are freeing yourself from bondage. If you permit yourself to remain emotionally stuck in a spot, you will spend your whole life related to that spot. Do you want your life tied to something that occurred when you were seven years old? What you are holding onto is a hurt.

Let us briefly think about hurt. Hurt! Somebody hurts you and you get angry. Genuine anger lasts only thirty seconds. After that it is an ego trip. Sometimes it is easier to wallow in hurt than it is to ask yourself if it is worth the amount of energy you are expending on it. So many times, all your energies get directed to the hurt. Everything will relate to it. "I can't eat lettuce because that was what was served that night." This is the kind of rationalization that begins to build upon hurt. Everything becomes focused on the hurt.

Now if all your energies are directed to hurt, the only thing that can be attracted into your life is hurt. You are your own magnet, so you can see what a mess you make for yourself along the way. When you focus in a painful space, you become suspect of others' actions, and there is a tendency to judge everything and everybody associated with the painful experience. It all boils down to this: Are you happy wallowing in hurt? If hurt is the most marvelous thing for you, stay there! Can you admit to yourself that perhaps this incident can serve you in another way? Look at it from all sides. Maybe you do not even know why you came to be in that position. Ask yourself the question, "Is the energy I am expending on it worth it?" If you cannot understand it, you will waste your whole life on an incident you do not understand. You have the power to say, I can convert that hurt by going to its opposite. You must begin to think painless thoughts. You begin to use your ability to release the hurt. You take away its ability to give you pain, because as *you* think, so shall it be.

Very often when you are frustrated or are unable to have an objective handle on a situation, you search for a way which will help you to feel better. It is called rationalization. You may even bring in past lives because that helps to make for good justification, and that too is rationalization. "I knew him in ancient Egypt, so I must be supposed to have an affair with him in this life."

Rationalization is a convenient and easy way of making things appear as you would like them to be without recognition of the objective realities that made them as they are. Past lives belong in the past. The only thing that comes forward from them is the essence of the emotion for recognition of the quality and knowledge gained from that point in time. If you were a dancer in ancient Egypt, you danced very differently from the dance of today. The essence of dance comes forward with you but not the steps. They belong to another culture and time.

Remember, when you have images from past lives, they only give you a perspective of where you *have been*. All direction and guidance that is meant to come to you does so through the high consciousness, your God-Self.

As you begin to develop and come to understand

27

yourself, it is very important for you to understand the role eye contact plays in your self-expression. When you look at someone, they know you have something to say. Say it clearly and with a low voice. If you are feeling angry, take a moment, take a deep breath, wait a minute and then go on calmly. It takes time and practice. The more you do it, the more you hear yourself heard.

When you are faced with a reality you cannot resolve, give it up to God. You will be amazed how relaxed you will become. You may occasionally from time to time feel it creeping back. When you see it coming back, treat it with humor. It is quite normal to have things try to come back. Scoop them out again. The point to remember is this: it is easy to forgive, but hard to forget. If you tie yourself to the past you cannot move forward in the present. If you keep letting an event from fourteen years ago come into the present, you are never going to move forward. Fourteen years ago you may have failed, but *love the way you are now.* Change the failure thought with an alternate thought. Bless it, laugh at it, but do not give it power.

The focus of all change in life is based on the formula that from the need comes the desire, from the desire—the participation, and from the participation—the fulfillment.

Physical expression is the means of saying look at me, hear me, see my needs. Physical expression can be most positive or it can be equally negative. It is possible to become competitive to the degree that to win becomes the most important point, that to *succeed* is more important than to *be.* Why do you want success? If you want success only to get that pat on the back, that is not enough. You have to want it because it will lead to greater use of *your* potential. This is what many people do not realize. Many of the moves you make in life are instigated not by your *inner reality* but by ego. Physical activity is a means of expressing energy. Energy is directed and focused by thought. Watch your thoughts!

Many people who cannot find recognition in any other way will find it through fantasy or dramatic expression. There is nothing wrong with needing to be the center of attention as long as it is kept in balance. They use these beautiful expressions to release the inner emotions that they have not been able to express in any other way.

What happened when you were young has an influence on how you view the need to be aggressive or the need to be passive. As a child you may have experienced the feeling of being different or separate. This has to do with experiencing different energies. You know you are thinking a different way. Separation comes from how you view yourself in relation to others. Have you ever had the experience of having dinner guests and you count how many heads? There are nine people here, so you set the table for nine, totally forgetting to count yourself. It is because when you are identifying with things outside yourself, there is the tendency to hold yourself separate from them. Thus, many times the child will see the family as something out there. He will not really clearly understand that he belongs to it. The other source of this feeling is a difference in energy within you. Realize that even though you are doing the same things, you are on a different frequency. You are seeing it and you are feeling it differently.

A child who has had a life of happy experiences will have casual memories of it. When you are experiencing happiness, you go along with it. You are thinking happy because you are happy. Happiness will attract more happiness, and until something comes along to rock the boat, nothing else will register with you.

Difficult emotional experiences in childhood often create a tendency to anchor yourself to those emotions. As you look back in time, realize that the amount of importance that you gave to an incident gives it power in your life. Many people have a hard time letting go of an emotional incident. Every time they think about it, they fall back into the well of it. One of the finest methods of handling it is to daily write down your feelings. Be frank and know that no one but you is going to read this. What you are doing is taking the emotion out of you and making it separate from yourself by putting it in another location. By doing that you are able to better handle it. If you can laugh at the self and with others, nothing in the world can stop you. It is only when one takes themselves too seriously, thinking they can not make a mistake, that they fail themselves. Think how vulnerable you are then.

Self-pity is self-abuse.

———————————————————Julian

**All creation is the same;
it is only perspective
that creates differences.**
—————————————————Julian

SELF-DISCOVERY

CHAPTER ★ IV

The Formation of The Child

A soul will very often make arrangements to be born into a certain family. Not every person in every life chooses his parents. Sometimes you say, give me the energy in a parent that is going to help my soul growth. When you do come into a life with a parent who has been with you before, that decision has been made before entering. The parent does not prepare to have you when you decide to enter the world. The parent prepares to have you before they are married to the person who is going to be the other parent. It is all preplanned. When all circumstances of energy are right, everything falls into place. There is one stumbling block—free will. The parents, once they are in the physical body and with conscious mind, are under the direction of free will. They can choose not to have a child.

The sex of a child is not preplanned. The sex of a child is biochemistry. The female egg is neuter and the male sperm determines the sex of the child. A spirit is neuter. It is neither male nor female. The spirit enters the body prepared for it. Gender is chosen by the male sperm and the female egg coming together. The spirit enters the fetus when the mother first feels life. The soul's lessons have nothing to do with whether you are male or female. Soul lessons have to do with how you handle the things presented to you in life. If it is a lesson in love, it does not matter whether the child is male or female.

A parent will, very often, out of their own psychic sense, be able to know their child's genetic development. If you are tuned in to the inner self, you know a lot more about what is going on with you than anyone realizes. There is no reason for you to be out of touch with any part of your body.

There is nothing that can stop the sperm and the egg from doing their thing. If your state of mind is the magnet that attracts to you, then you can have an influence on what is happening. It is amazing. When two people are attuned strongly, they will be able to tell you exactly when conception took place because they are so in tune with the bodies. They know the moment the merger occurs.

You are an aware being when you enter the world. There is a shock at birth because you are experiencing for the first time the total physical separation from your mother. You move from her temple into your own temple. Birth creates the first realization of physical separation. It is also the movement toward independence upon which all of your life is based.

What you feel in the womb is still the spiritual awareness factor, not the physical/emotional factor. The attitude and the emotions of the mother and her environment are sensed while still in the womb. This is through the awareness factor and it is not an emotional experience. Once the child is born it begins to feel with physical emotion.

There are sometimes gender prejudices. If a parent is told they are going to have a male when they wanted a female or vice versa, there can be a resentment built up toward the child. The child is going to be aware of this conflict of emotions the whole time it is being carried. Once the child is born and the mother or father hold it, it does not matter what sex it is. The prejudice is wiped out. The child has not had a period of feeling rejected.

A child needs mothering, nurturing, and love; but it does not always get it from the person who bears it. As long as there is someone who will love it, nurture it, and give it the feeling of security, it will respond. This is because the child is open and aware when it is born. It is ready to be loved even though it has sensed being unloved in the womb.

Wonderful things can happen to a child who was not wanted before birth. When he first appears, those attitudes change; there is the realization of how lovable this child is. Those negative feelings that surrounded it previously can be altered. A child who is held, whether it is by the mother who bore it or anyone else, will respond to beauty and love around it.

Remember that concepts of love are formed from your first breath as a child. Concepts are formed while you are still in the womb. A child knows what it is being born into. The woman who carries a child and does not want it will bear a child who knows it.

If a child does not receive the nurturing love it needs, those feelings of being unloved will be held by the child. It will carry those feelings until an age of aggression. Seven is the first breaking point, fourteen is the next, and twenty-one, and every seven years thereafter. Hopefully, comprehension comes over those years which helps the child to see that in some instances a child, unwanted at birth, can become a very special person. They recognize that the situation exists, but it is not because of anything *they* have caused. By taking that acceptance into themselves, they can forgive the act of un-love and move forward in love, be loving themselves and *of* themselves.

The children who come in during this age, called the Aquarian Age, will not be willing to let go of the natural awareness they were born with. They are going to hold on to their identity from the very beginning. The seven-year cycles will still apply, but there will not be the need for the same aggression. They will not be trying to recapture something that they had a sense of losing. Their awareness factor will be held onto because of the very energy of the time that they are functioning in. Their parents are going to become more aware of the need to keep the child open to his full potential.

It is important for you to understand the seven-year cycle aggression. *The soul's urge, the soul's push* to create change in your life for your benefit and your progress is very often interpreted as negative aggression. It is seen as an aggression because it appears to be changing everything as you have understood it, up to that point in your life. Therefore, an aggressive feeling comes from the gentle push of the soul. That aggression must then be brought into balance and controlled in order for it to bring the child the fullest reward.

**The next time you decide
to make yourself over,
be daring—
try a new pattern.**

———————————————————————Julian

Observe nature well; it is a magnificent teacher.

————————————————Julian

CHAPTER ★ V

Child-Parent Relationships

The children born during this age will have to grow up physically to match the mental, emotional, and spiritual awareness that is there. They will remain more in tune with the universal consciousness. They are open enough at that young age to know things that by all learning experiences, they could not know. No matter how aware they are, they are guided, shaped, and molded by those who govern them. The thing that all parents must understand is that children are on loan to them. They are not owned, they are loaned. You get the opportunity to guide them through constructive formative times.

During your young childhood years you associate incidents and words with emotions. Sometimes you become hung up on them; other times you recognize it for what it is and are able to move into a new understanding of that incident. If I asked you what is fun, each of you would have your own opinion of what fun would be. To one person a good time would be going out and getting intoxicated and later having a hangover. That is their fun! To another person it would be sitting at home reading a really good book or going out to see a magnificent performance. Fun is a matter of preference, and it is seen through the individual's value system. A child who has longed to do something and been told it is not nice may later in life find himself feeling guilty about having fun in that way. In this manner there is a tendency to make fun a form of self-punishment. I want to let you begin to understand how you tie associations and emotions.

What we feel around us feeds our fantasies which, in turn, feed our creative thoughts and gives direction to them. A child surrounded by a disturbing situation which he does not understand can begin to fantasize. This can often lead to a conflict about how he sees love in his life. The same kind of conflict can occur from being surrounded by very loving incidents or from being surrounded by very traumatic incidents. They are the two ends of the pole, each a polarity of the other. A person who is very loved may sometimes begin to feel smothered. It does not matter whether it is a child-parent relationship, husband-wife, or whatever. Somewhere in between they have to create the balance.

The mother's love can become smother-love if it denies independence or decision making to the child. This is also true of the father. The balance has to be there, the give and the take. You have to watch what the balance is in that giving. How is another reacting to it? If a person's needs are not understood, you may be smothering them with that giving or loving. They may not be able to handle that much. That is why communication is the most vital thing in a relationship. If a person does not let their needs be known, they cannot be answered.

When there has been a disagreement and it has led to a separation or a walking out of one of the parents, the child feels walked out on. The child feels guilt because the child is not quite able to handle the fact that the two loving beings who brought him into the world will not be there anymore as a couple. The child sees it as something he has done wrong.

When such an incident has occurred, it is important that the child realizes that sometimes grown-ups find they do not get along well together. It is better for them to be apart and, therefore, better for the child. One of the strangest statements in your world is, "We stayed together for the sake of the children." The children grow up with anger, hatred, coldness, and a confusion. "Why? What have I done?" The only thing they have to relate to is themselves. It is far better to give an explanation than it is to hope that if you ignore the situation, it will go away. The negativity will remain and will have to be expressed in some way. An uncontrolled situation will manifest an uncontrolled attitude in you.

In an adoption, the child is very often adopted by the ones who are meant to be the parents. The manner in which this comes about also frees some kind of karmic relationship with the natural mother. This is not in every case but does hold in *most* cases. In the majority of cases, however, it is answering more than one avenue of soul growth, both that of the child as well as those who adopt and those who must let the child go. There is a tendency always to think that the parents who give the child up are some kind of ogres. This often overlooks the possibility of circumstances where the child has more of a chance by the parents releasing them. I am not talking of incidents where somebody finds themselves pregnant and says, "Oh, what the hell, I'll have it," and then they give the child away. I am talking about those who agonize over their inability emotionally, financially, or whatever, to care for the child and give that child up for adoption, hoping that it will give the child more. Love one another unconditionally. Do not judge.

How a child has viewed the male/female relationship through its parents will greatly influence its aggressive expression later during the fourteen- and twenty-one-year cycles. It is important to realize the male parent is equally important as the female parent to the child. The child is a polarity of both parents, and that polarity will have an expression and a need to be fulfilled. How you are shaped and molded during a seven-year cycle will determine how you will benefit in each succeeding seven-year cycle. At every seven-year unfoldment within the self, according to how much you are still listening to the reality self, there is a new discovery and a new unfoldment of everything about you.

Aggressiveness in a child has to be controlled. The thing that the child decides is right for himself may be something about which he is not yet able to make a good decision. There are times when a parent has to say no, but it should be done without creating a war. That is literally what often happens—you begin an inner war. There is a smile on the outside, but inside there is turmoil.

When a child says no, do you realize what a shock it is to the parent? "My sweet, docile child who took every word I said as gospel suddenly says, 'No.'" Adults are really shaken by that. The natural instinct is to control the situation. Just as an uncontrolled situation in the child created trauma, an uncontrolled situation for the adult creates stress. You must get your point across, but not let anger intervene. It is not easy. Do not expect a child to understand the emotional trauma *you* are going through. All they can understand is the fact that they feel the pain of it, and sometimes you have to say to a child, "Look, I am not in the best of moods today; bear with it." A child can understand that there are days when you do not feel good. This is far better than being barked at every two minutes when they do not know why.

One of the greatest gifts a child has is the ability to think creatively and to fantasize. In the first seven years you play make-believe. In the second seven years you fantasize and daydream. In the third seven-year period you take the fantasy and the daydream and begin to put them into creative form. You shape and mold what has been fantasy into creative thoughts that can make them happen.

One of the problems in your world today is the removal of creative instincts in children by toys that do it all. Children who can take blocks and make castles, or dungeons, or whatever they want from them are using their inner creative instincts. Have you ever noticed that a very young child will end up playing with the boxes that the toy came in? The inner instinct says, "I can do it. I can make it. I do not have to rely on something else, doing it for me." They are still holding on to a shred of themselves. When children are denied the opportunity for, or restricted from, creative play, the frustration can create anger. This can also happen to adults.

Interaction between parent and child on a creative level is important. There are many ways to do this. Reading to a child is a very intimate thing. It takes a space in time and puts you and the child together with whatever fantasy is being experienced from that book. It is a happy experience. You go into a special place with someone else and share a marvelous thing. Whatever it is, the fact is that it is a fantasy just for you. It is like having a private show. The seed for creative thought is also formed. Children need to learn that their minds are important. How they think matters.

Teach your children to understand the power that they wield when they direct their energies to another. Teach your children how important it is to realize that if they direct that power to hurt and harm another, they will have to have that hurt come back to them. It might not be right away, but it is going to come, because the law of cause and effect says it will. Help your children understand that they are creating their destiny, and they must work to bring the right destiny to themselves.

Remember, that...
whatever you send out is
going to come back—
to roost on your doorstep.
—Julian

If you keep telling the same stories over and over, maybe it is time for some new adventures.

—Julian

CHAPTER ★ VI

Adult Relationships

Many people enter into relationships and experience a cosmic, mystical thing. Yet, all the while they are enjoying it, there is that feeling that it will either not last or that they may lose this wonderful person to another. That is an insecurity within the self. This is an insecurity that says, "I am not worthy of holding it."

Frequently, insecurity within the self creates a feeling of unworthiness. You would not be able to be in a fine relationship if you were not worthy. You must permit yourself to joyously give and receive in that relationship. Do not ruin the joy of the moment with fear of the future. Remember that your thoughts have the power of creation. Let your thoughts be of happiness and lasting love. That can then manifest. To think differently is to taint the love aspect of the present. Do not worry about tomorrow or the next day, enjoy today. If you are so busy looking for a reason that today cannot be happy, those thoughts are going to manifest and cut off the positive good you hope to achieve.

At every point in your life, you are open to new and marvelous things. You must always be willing to go with the change, even in relationships. If you block them from the beginning by fear of losing them, you will never have the chance to have them move with you. Accept that it is okay and enjoy it.

There is nothing in life that is not meant to be enjoyed. Everyone seems to think that love has to be extremely painful. Some of it is. It is a healthy pain. The child who is growing up and leaving the home hurts. It is a good pain because the child is coming into its own.

Recognize that life is a flow. Move with it and enjoy each space in that movement. Do not fear the future, for you will have everything you are meant to have. You are not going to be a loser because one relationship ends. Think of the better ones to come. Remember, you were meant to be you and to be fulfilled in the manner right for you.

The essence of love is universal; it permeates all things. The body chemistry reaction of love is strictly of the physical, and unless the essence of love beyond that is there, it will be short-lived. The love on many levels has to be there to have a lasting relationship.

People love for many different reasons—body chemistry, needs being fulfilled, a chance to give. Many different things enter a love relationship, but it has to function on more than just body chemistry in order to last.

If you feel good about yourself, you can share that goodness with another, and you can laugh at the weaknesses because love is strong. Love is the strongest energy in the universe. The world was created in love and of love, and it is the strongest energy that exists.

If love is personalized to the degree of ego, it gets to be a check list and can have a destructive aspect. I have seen many times in your world where someone will feel totally rejected because a friend will criticize their choice of clothing. A person wearing their favorite shirt may interpret this criticism of their choice of clothing as an attack. By personalizing this feeling, they develop anger, resentment, and hurt. It does not matter if others do not agree with you or would prefer to see you differently. A non-personal attitude permits you to accept that they may prefer a different shirt on you, while you go on totally enjoying the one you are wearing.

You have to be very careful that you are not taking an energy that is supposed to function universally and personalizing it by ego. I have seen incidents where somebody has made a statement about something in a meeting, and later, one of the persons in that room has thought that every statement in there was directed at them. Because of ego interpretation, everything that was said was being personalized.

The opposite polarity of the ego is the lack of self-esteem. If my ego is not saying that I am the greatest, perhaps the other polarity that is in operation says I am not worth anything, so nobody could possibly agree with me. You have to find that point between the two extremes. It is okay to disagree. It is okay to have different interests. It means being your own person. Do not make a personal issue out of a casual statement. Be you, but be open to communication.

You have to maintain yourself as a whole being and, from that wholeness, share yourself. Know that you are not going to be identical in all things. If everybody breathed in and out at the same time, there would be no rhythm, just a great suction. You have to understand that variety is necessary, and it is necessary to permit yourself to be yourself. Respect yourself! Really know who you are. We are talking about knowing what your needs are and being willing to know and express them. You need to be willing to listen to the needs of another and express to them your needs. It is not a checklist or a tug-of-war, but an *acceptance*.

Remember that key word "acceptance." Through acceptance you are able to have a relationship that is a sharing.

Love is an acceptance of each other as you are at that time and moment. The only thing that is absolute in the world is change, and that is something that has to be recognized. There is not a person who can remain the same. If nothing else, they become more fixed in whatever their particular belief.

At all points in a relationship, communication is absolutely the most important aspect of it. Not communication after the fact, not communication that says yesterday you did this or that, but communication that says "These are my needs." It is *non-defensive* communication. It is a communication that says "I love you," but does not mean that one lies down and becomes a door mat. Love is sharing; it is sharing *both* the good and the bad.

Realize that how you think about a relationship, or anything in your life, will determine its length. A person who has a new relationship or a new job and immediately fears that he is going to lose it will drive it away. That is because a form of distrust and rejection is emanating from them.

Realize that acceptance of yourself permits your acceptance of any situation in relationship to yourself. If I am enough in myself, the relationship will be enough for me, or the job will be enough for me. The fear immediately begins to project a pushing away or a distrust of your ability to have it. It is very important always to recognize that the moment something is yours, you must accept it rightfully and know that you have earned it. Do not fear that it is not going to be yours again. Very often in life, one blocks something marvelous coming to them because they are afraid. They are afraid they are missing something else, so they hold on to what they have because they think nothing else can be theirs, and as a result, nothing else is.

You must recognize that people outgrow each other. Friendships outgrow each other. You do not stop caring, you do not stop loving, but recognize that you sometimes take different roads and separate paths. That does not mean that you are less of a being.

When you are involved in a relationship and the other person changes or wants to change, you have to ask yourself how valid it is. And what is going on that needs change. Is that change right for you? When somebody else starts to say, "It is not working any more," you have to honestly look at yourself and ask "Why?" You may be placidly happy with it, but totally unaware of what you are causing for somebody else. You have to take a good look at where they are coming from, where you are coming from, and see what is happening with the relationship.

A relationship has to move. A relationship cannot stay the same because change is absolute. The first feelings of love are nothing like those felt at the twenty-fifth wedding anniversary, but both are expressions of love. It is a different movement in the time of the relationship. A relationship that tries to make it in one spot and never move is going to find friction sooner or later. You have to move with it, and you have to look at it and say, "Okay. Why?" Try to see what is happening there.

People very often think that a difference in age places them in different phases of these cycles. It does not. A relationship is of two whole people sharing. As long as both people are sharing in the relationship and are totally conscious of what it means on all levels, there will be no cause for concern. Age is a state of mind. I have known many seven-year-olds who are seventeen and many twenty-year-olds who are one hundred.

Age is a state of mind, and the body follows the mind. The body will reflect the mental attitudes. Therefore, it is the belief systems of the people in the relationship which cause them to separate or remain together. If two people are honestly looking at each other and accepting each other on all levels, they will share totally. It is not only a mental attitude, it is the whole being sharing. If they can achieve that, they can have an extremely successful relationship.

If a fourteen-year-old marries a seventeen-year-old, it is a close union in age, but with immaturity on both sides. It is bound to lead to trouble because neither one knows yet who they really are. The ingredients that are put into any relationship are going to be the form and dance the relationship has. There are no specifics for a relationship. Many relationships in the world function with great age discrepancies and are very happy ones. A relationship deals with the people in it and how ready they are themselves.

A relationship that is based on one person becoming the other will fail. If you think that you are going to win a relationship by permitting yourself to become the mirror image of the person you are with, you are wrong. Once you have permitted your unique individuality to be swallowed by another personality, you, in essence, are no longer there. The very thing that attracted this person to you will be missing. Two things occur: first, you begin to resent being lost; and second, they begin to feel you have changed. At the next aggression cycle for either party, resentment will be shown.

Conflicts in relationships very often result from failure to communicate needs. The most important thing is to let the other person know your needs. If a person does not know what you need, there is no way on earth that they can ever answer them. I have so often heard people in your world say, "If he loved me, he would know!" Not if you're A and he is B. There is no way that A and B will think alike, but if they tell each other what they need, they will have a chance. There is *no way* you can *demand* that another show you love your way. *You can* let them know what your needs are. *You can* ask them what their needs are. Be loving to be loving, but not to change another. Many times I have found that difficulties exist because one is projecting an image that is not the other's reality. You have to ask questions and work with what is the reality there, not your fantasy.

Self-discovery is a step-by-step evolution, but many times it can take a quantum leap. Sometimes a single realization crosses all the barriers. Sometimes a single realization about the self releases a whole new thing. I will give you a perfect example. Recently a young couple, newly in love, went away on a vacation together. They did all the things that you are supposed to do on a vacation. They came back, and on the last day, sitting together, they said, "Next time we have a vacation, let's stay home." Both of them admitted at that point that they really did not like running around. They would have been much more at ease staying at home, getting to know each other, and doing simple things about the home that they liked to do. Do you realize what a wonderful insight that singular thing is to their whole future relationship? No longer do they have to worry where the other will want to go for vacation. They are both content to be wherever they are. That is a tremendous realization.

You are very often presented with conflicts in a relationship which cause you to question whether it should continue. Trying to understand whether you should remain with a relationship or let go requires you to have an introspection or meditation with yourself. Ask yourself why you are hanging in—from habit? A bird in hand is worth two in the bush sort of thing? Are you afraid of the unknown if you do not have that relationship? What will people think? In your world, you have always let other people's opinions shape and mold your ability to be. You value yourself by other people's opinions. Then along comes a situation where you have to go against what you think other people might like, and you become terrified. What is the world of reality? Where does your reality fit into this? If a relationship is becoming a detriment to the spiritual growth or harmful to the physical and mental being, it is no longer a relationship. It is time to let it go to a new perspective.

To end a relationship is not bad as long as it is done lovingly. It is only when a relationship ends with hatred and vengeance, which is all ego-bound, that you are being detrimental to the self. Naturally, it is not wise to say, "I am going to end this relationship because I do not want it any more. Mother and the six children can starve." You are going to have karma from that one. There has to be a logic to your thinking. You must also remember that if you have become a lesser being by a relationship, the relationship is not serving a purpose that is to your or the other's benefit. If another person is learning cruelty, or to be an egotist, then it is a detriment to them as well. You must ask why you want to end it or where you want the relationship to go, for only you can decide what is right and proper for you.

Everyone loves universally. Universal love is based on the spiritual level. People love their mother, their children, their spouse, their lover. They are all love, but they are all different energy packages or expressions of that love, and they each have different anticipations.

Unconditional love has nothing to do with physical love. It is the love that sustains a person. It lets you recognize the good in a person, even when you have outgrown that person, or feel a need to let go of that person. It is the thing that lets divorce happen without hatred. That is unconditional love. It is the love that says, we may not belong together anymore, we may not be able to answer each others needs, but we do not have to hate each other.

Unconditional love does not mean becoming a doormat. It does not mean laying yourself down and letting everybody walk all over you. It means to be willing to recognize that even in a person who distresses you greatly, there is good. "The God in me recognizes the God in you and wishes it well."

You must be careful that the anticipation of the love is not a fantasy projection of yours alone. It has to be a sharing, two whole people sharing, never a domination, never a leeching. Many times in a love relationship, a fantasy image is projected upon another, and when that anticipation fails, they think the person has failed them. All the person has done is be themselves. You have to understand what it is you really expect from this person when you are in a relationship. "Is it a reality for both of us, or is it just an expectation of mine?" You must let your expectations be known; otherwise, they will never be fulfilled. One does love on many levels within a relationship and in many ways surrounding that relationship.

When you leave yourself open to someone emotionally or sexually, you are opening yourself to being vulnerable. When you become vulnerable, you are not in control, and when you are not in control, it worries you. It becomes a point of concern. Know yourself and then you know whether you want to be vulnerable. You do not put yourself in vulnerable positions because the "almighty" *"they"* are doing it.

I will say this to you: Your ability to love is within yourself. Unless you love yourself, you will never love another. You will try, but you will always fail; for only within you is the ability to love, and only by nurturing that can you nurture it in another. The first person you have to like and love is *you*. That is not self-centeredness; it is not selfishness; it is reality. If you have trouble loving yourself, begin by looking at yourself in the mirror, eye-to-eye, and saying, "I love you."

You have to know with a certainty what you deem love. Otherwise, it gets to be, Mrs. Jones says, "Love is this. He does everything you want, or else he does not love you." This may seem farfetched, but suppose he has the same idea. The two of you are never going to get anywhere. You have to ask what love is to you in your own reality, not what everyone else says it is. Some people can be totally happy catering to another person's needs. That fulfills them and makes them feel rich and wonderful. They love every moment of it. Another person may be so fed up with it by day two that they are ready to call it quits. In your world, there is the tendency to try to become the other person. If I love him, I will immediately like to eat oysters, clams or whatever. I will immediately ski, even though I have never been on the slopes in my life. You are becoming the mirror image of somebody else. Sooner or later you are going to revolt and say, "What about me? What happens to me?" And then you are going to have trouble. You have to be yourself and be willing to share yourself in order to have a relationship.

It is quite possible to love someone and not like them, because there may be attitudes of that person's personality or character that momentarily irritate you. On a deeper level, you know what is there and you love them. You love your children, but you certainly do not like them all the time (if you are honest with yourself). It is all right to say, I do not like what you are doing right now. When you tell your children that you do not like them, be sure to tell them you love them.

You often face situations and involvements with others that are extremely negative. Very often you may desire to change or alter a person, especially if you live with them. Be careful. The goal of life should never be to change the person. The goal of life should be to see what needs to be changed in *you* in order to be able to *see* the person. In your world, I see, time and time again, people coming together for all the wrong reasons. While claiming to be in perfect accord, in the back of the mind rests the thought that once we are solidified, he or she will change. If you succeed in changing the other, the union will end, because what you were attracted to in the first place will be killed—it will be gone. What happens is a modification *from both*. There are times when people are very, very negative and nothing is going to change them, because they do not even see that they are negative. They have come up thinking the glass is half empty instead of half full. If there is a gloomy side they will take it. You must not permit that atmosphere to be yours. You must remain the point of light within darkness.

You do this by knowing your value, knowing your worth, and being willing to be you, whether that person approves of you or not. When you are surrounded by negativity that refuses to break in any way (by "break" I mean modify), re-evaluate the situation. One must not capitulate to the other, that is domination. Understand also that you can dominate by weakness just as well as you can dominate by strength. Have you ever noticed that if there is a weak person in a room, everybody else caters to him? If there is somebody hammering their fist on the table, everybody is listening. You must keep the point of light in yourself. You must not permit yourself to become negative.

When you are surrounded by people who are always negative and will not change, you accept them as they are. By accepting them as they are, you are releasing yourself from judgment, which is a karmic attachment to that person. You do not have to like them, but you do have to love them. You have to accept them as they are. You have to accept that that is their divine right of discernment. If they want to go around being negative, you do not have to accept the energy of it. You release yourself from karma by not being the judge. You have the right to say, "I do not *like* what you do. I do not *like* what you are involved in. I do not *like* your attitude. I would really feel happier if it were not a part of me." You detach yourself from them, you bless them, and let them go their way. There is the expression "turn the other cheek." It does not mean turn it so it gets hurt. It means turn away from the energy that has been the offender. Change the energy that created the situation. Turn to the opposite energy. Above all, do not get caught up being judgmental, because then you are tied to it.

When you are dealing with life in a detached manner, you are dealing with facts rather than emotions. It does not mean that you do not feel sorry for the unfortunate around you. You just do not join in their misfortune. You extend compassion. When you have done all that you can do for a person, the only thing left for you to do is become compassionate. Hold them in light that they may be supported in energy to withstand or control their affliction as best they can. Do not wallow in something with someone, or you add to the negativity of the situation. One person bewailing something is one thing, ten bewailing it is quite another. One must say, "I feel for you. I have empathy, but what are you going to do about it?" If in trying to help, your efforts are not enough or are rejected, you must still have compassion. Do not become disappointed if they do not listen to you or do what was suggested. Do not join their rejection energy; remain positive. In that situation you say, "Okay, my practical help as I see it was not enough. Now I shall pray, I shall bless them, I shall love them, and I shall care for them." Do not assume that everybody else is similarly detached.

People have to go to the reality of themselves. They have to know that there are no half packages, that whatever their decision is, they have to accept the full package of that decision. For example, in an intercultural relationship, both parties are going to have to accept that not everybody is going to approve. They are going to have to accept all the flack that comes with it. If their love is strong enough they will survive it. It is not a case of what makes the relationship happen, but how they direct the energy of the relationship. Can they accept the full responsibility of their decision?

A relationship occurs between two people and regardless of outside influences—cultural, family, or whatever— *they* must determine inside themselves what they are going to do. They must make their move and accept whatever comes from it. If they are going by their own inner self, they will enjoy a successful relationship.

Very often in a relationship, one will give and give until they make the other person uneasy. If you are the giver, you have to ask yourself why you are giving. If that giving is creating discomfort for you or the other person, it is out of balance. You may be giving because you think you have to, or because you feel giving is the only thing that makes you acceptable. There are times when too much giving will cause the recipient to become uneasy or feel dominated by it all. This may be especially so if the other person is not in a position to return the giving. If you have permitted giving to get out of balance to where it has become a negative, you have to bring it back into balance.

If a person has given to the point of imbalance and feels used, then they may find it difficult to give in the next situation. Your pendulum has swung from one extreme to the other. You must gradually come to the apex point, or midpoint to balance. In order to do so, you must permit yourself to give. It does not have to be in the same manner, but permit yourself to give. It can be time, energy, or a book. Permit yourself to give in some way. You are going to have to bring the pendulum that has swung too far one way back to its balance point.

People give, but they have a silent string attached to it. They think they do not, but they do. They are expecting something in return, whether they realize it or not. If that does not materialize, then all of a sudden, they feel used. They feel taken advantage of and then the tendency is to go the other way. Go into yourself and ask to have the right and proper balance in your giving. Feel free to give without getting. Do not give just to get. Remember also that the law of polarity says you must also permit yourself to receive. That is balance, for you cannot deny someone else the gift of giving.

Balance is the harmony between two points. Remember your polarities and the apex point which is the balance between the two. Every person sees what is happening from their own view point, so judgment cannot be made as to who is right and who is wrong. The balance has to be kept in each situation. A person who is willing to give a great deal may sometimes be totally content with themselves. They do not feel that anything is being taken away from them in the giving. Others may be giving because they think that is the only way to gain any kind of self-esteem. The reason giving is going on and to what degree is important. Giving to a degree that endangers the self is a negative. It is important always to keep the balance in this area.

There are some people who are happy giving to others totally. There are some who cannot. It is balance that should be kept. The person who gives to the detriment of self has turned a positive into a negative. If you give until you drop dead of exhaustion, you have made a negative. If you take until you are hurting others, it is a negative.

The factors that motivate one's behavior result from a diverse variety of influences. Sometimes people will do something purely to be contrary to what others expect of them. Others are overly concerned that their behavior conform to what they believe others expect of them. In either case the root of their behavior is motivated by influences which are outside themselves. The degree of their maturity at any point in the life determines their ability to handle things. Many times people marry too young and are unable to handle the emotions. They separate, and later, they might choose to remarry at a more mature age. They then are able to handle the emotion.

People hold on to negatives because they are afraid of having a void in their life. When they let that negative go what do they do next? What is going to fill that space? Sit down and talk with yourself. Ask what value it really has in your life *now*. Are you directing too much energy to the negative when that energy could be used in a positive manner instead? Put it on a mental scale and work from there. Any thing that becomes too much becomes negative. The person who constantly gives denies the gift of giving to someone else. There has to be the getting as well. In everything there is the balance between the two. To give is good, but you have to watch what effect the giving is having.

Let each experience be a growing, learning thing for you and move on with it. Do not be afraid to give. Know that you are lovable, whether anyone is *giving to you or not*. It has to be recognized that when you accept a gift of any kind, you are giving the gift of giving to someone else. You are also accepting your own worth. That exchange is very important, but very often out of a need, an insecurity, or desire to prove that you are loving, there is a tendency to want to do it all.

You are a being. You will bring from that being, through love and through interaction, a sense of well-being that will make you able to say, "I am and that is enough. I am capable of sharing that with others on all different levels." Do not manifest thoughts such as, "I cannot be because I do not have . . . ." or "I cannot be because no one has recognized me." The unions that survive are those that give space to the individual. Those that try to dominate or leech will fail. Only when you realize that you are enough can you let another person be themselves. You are then able to survive separateness. It is unity, caring, and love that create the strong foundation which lets each person be himself. A person happy with himself can truly accept himself. They are not going to be put down when somebody does not agree with them. They are not going to be put down when somebody has a different opinion or a different interest. There will be no need to put someone else down.

Do not wait to tell your children, your spouse, or your friends that you love them. Do it *now*. This is universal. That is breaking walls and barriers. When you are in a situation in your life that really needs change, the first stage is to question where it really needs change. Does my attitude toward it need changing? There are many incidents in your life when something occurs that seems to be very negative or seems to be a great inconvenience. Later, you find out they have saved your life. The forgotten thing that you return to get may be what keeps you off the highway at a specific moment and at a specific place. Any event that happens in your life should be looked at as a value and not as a negative. See in it a chance to grow. Work with it from the viewpoint of its effect on you and your relationship to it, not from the viewpoint of what people are going to think.

**It does not matter
whether an incident was right
or wrong, good or bad,
fair or not fair; it happened.
Look at the facts,
learn from them, and move on.**

——————————————————————————————Julian

Your energy is like money. It is best not to spend more than you have. When you overspend, you lose.

——Julian

CHAPTER ★ VII

Focusing Your Energy

When an incident in life is giving you a problem, instead of wasting energy on the problem, ask yourself why it is a problem. Is it really a problem, or is it a problem because somebody says it is? This is fine if you wish to agree with everybody else. Suppose they think it is a problem but you do not? What do you do then? At that point, you have to make a decision about this issue and how important it is in your life. Is it worth all the energy that you are expending on it? Unless you can make that decision, you will get nowhere with the problem. You have to know how important it is, and how much energy it has the right to take from you.

You can find yourself in a position where you have been manipulated by others into thinking that you have to do something about it. Are your decisions based on you, or are they based on what other people say? Over fifty per cent of all decisions made in your universe are usually based on other people's criteria, rather than on those of the individual involved. There is always outside influence; there are always other people's opinions; and there are always the rules and regulations of the culture. They do influence you and you do interact with them. When ultimately the question comes up about you, you must go inward to the inner self and ask yourself, "What is my reality? What is right for me?" You must answer to your reality. Far too many times, one responds with a passive attitude of let's not "rock the boat." If you do not state how you feel, then you do not have the right to complain about it later. Have you ever noticed how things usually go in a meeting? The opinions are asked for, but nobody says a word. Immediately after the meeting, there are knots of people in various corners of the corridors all talking about what they really wanted to do. They, however, did nothing. How can anything be accomplished unless you know what you stand for?

Be willing to stand up for what you believe in. In all phases of your life, you must believe in *you*. You must not be afraid to let your aggression show. However, show it in a controlled manner, not in a temper tantrum. Express it in a way that says, I have thought about it, and this is the way I feel. Every incident that is expressed by aggressive anger will be treated as a temper tantrum. Those things that are expressed by an assertive statement will hold weight. A statement delivered calmly, clearly, and with the realization that it is what you really believe will be listened to. The more you lower your voice, the more others are apt to listen. There is no need to push it. All too often, a raised voice is interpreted as a forced issue. It is considered an attempt to make somebody accept that which they do not want.

When an idea is clearly and calmly stated, it will be listened to much more readily. If you think of different incidents in your life when you have felt put upon or annoyed, they probably have been because of a raised voice. Why? Because your own aggressiveness, with a need to be interpreted, is being smothered by an act of force. Conversation permits a difference of opinion and a difference of ideas without a danger; shouting matches always end with upsets. Know yourself, know what you stand for, and be willing to state it. The greatest act of faith is to say something contrary to what everybody else agrees with. Be willing to be what you are, who you are, and what you stand for. The whole objective of this book is to prepare you for working with different energies. It is to bring you into balance, into an understanding about how *you* feel about *you*, to help you know *your* value and *your* worth, and to enable you to work with it.

I would like you to repeat a simple statement: *I am, and I am enough.* You are enough to achieve, through your potential, anything you want to achieve. Potential blossoms by action. If you want to paint, paint! What makes you start painting? A blank canvas? No. Shut your eyes and put a mark on it, it is no longer a blank. In your world I constantly hear, "I always wanted to . . ." or "I wish I had . . ." and "Someday I am going to . . ." If you wish to draw, draw every day. If you wish to dance, dance every day. If you cannot dance with your feet, dance with your head. If you are riding the bus you can still dance with your head. Do not wait for the magic day when it is all going to fall into place. You are all kidding yourselves. You have got to go through the stumbling blocks of learning to draw, dance, or paint.

The only way you are going to do it is to familiarize yourself with it. You familiarize yourself with it by first knowing the tools. A dancer has to exercise. Those muscles and tendons have to respond. The painter has to know color. The person who is going to draw has to know how to sharpen the pencil. Start where you are. Work with it in a manner available to you presently. Let it grow in you to something more. Do not keep putting it off, because you will come to the very end and you will still not have done it. How wonderful to look back and say, "I did it." Later you may change your mind and your direction about it. This is better than saying, "I always wanted to do it but never got to it." It should be that way with everything in your life.

Recognize as you develop that many times, there are pitfalls along the way. There are some artists who become so attached to their work, so caught up in it, that part of them does not want to let it go. When they do not want to let it go, it cannot go out to make room for anything to come in. There has to be an attitude of prosperity flowing, and they must see the painting also as a prosperity flowing. Furthermore, the principle and the essence of painting depends on the quality given to it by mental direction. The artist may manifest a fine painting, but if his attitude is that no one would want it, then no one is going to. He has to be able to look at his painting and say, "This is the best I can do right now; let it go out and sell. I will do better the next time."

Merely focusing on painting, or any other career activity, of itself is not sufficient to assure you of a rewarding economic existence unless that has been a focus in the life. He who thinks he cannot have it, will not receive it. For the artist, painting a beautiful picture does not guarantee a monetary return unless there is a prosperity attitude in the whole life. What is the most common image you have of an artist? Someone starving in a garret. If that imagery is the essence of the artist's experience, then it is going to promulgate itself in the artist's life. The artist must see his paintings as a moving, flowing thing. The painter must understand that when he is not satisfied, it is an incentive for him to do better. Do not make the statement that becomes a blockage to the flow.

"I have failed." I have seen a six-year-old cry bitterly and say that he has failed. Poor thing has not had the chance to know what life is and already he has failed. Failure was programmed into that child. The point is this: you are all individuals, you are all humans with human emotions and human needs. You all, at times, have problems interacting with other people. Understand that this is quite normal. It does not mean that you have failed. It does not mean that you are wrong. It means two energies are acting as a repulsion rather than as an attraction. There is nothing negative in this. They are different energies interacting on different levels. The point is to build upon yourself and know that is enough. Interact with those who interact well with you. The grass always seems greener on the other side of the fence. "I have this, but do I really think that might be better?" You never have time to enjoy what you have, because you are always looking for what you might have missed, or what might be better. If I were to give you one thought to know about yourself, I would say stand still where you are and enjoy it! Stand still right where you are and enjoy it! Do not try to make it into something else until you have a chance to enjoy what you have.

Do not make the whole life a competition. Instead, let it be an outing and enjoy it. If there were no one to appreciate art, an artist would not have the fulfillment that he needs. If there were no one to read, there would be no need to write. Take time to see that you have a value in your own capacity. Just think of what your words mean to somebody else.

When facing a problem in life, you ask yourself how much value does this have in my life? For instance, you may feel your weight is becoming a problem. Ask yourself if this is the only thing that makes you valid. Perhaps too much attention is being paid to weight and more attention should be paid to thin. It takes time for the subconscious to accept these new attitudes as fact. The only way the subconscious has of accepting it is by repetition. You must keep telling it so. Be careful how you word it. If you are wording it in a manner that seems to be depriving you, you may find yourself resenting it.

The pituitary gland rules the body. It is the master gland of the body. The pineal gland is the master gland of the spirit body. When the subconscious releases to the body, it must release through the pituitary. It becomes the communication center of the body's emotions. The thought pattern creates the movement which creates the chemical change in the body.

The process of releasing is a repetitious series of events. It begins with you telling yourself, *"I release it and I bless it."* The more you say it, the sooner the subconscious accepts it and releases to your body the feeling of release. You have to work with the feeling through the subconscious mind and the pituitary gland to bring it to where the body can accept it.

When you are in emotional turmoil, the need to release is strong. This can be done through meditation or by writing it down. In meditation, you relate to the problem, and in writing it down, you make it separate from you so that you may see it more clearly. Now it is out of you. You are not generating a magnet that attracts it to you or gives it energy. You are looking at it as a separate energy and saying, "What can I do about this?" It then begins to fall into proper perspective and you are able to work with it. If you are not feeding it, it will not well up in the emotion of the self. It will have a chance to lower its energy enough to be seen and to dissipate.

When you cannot handle a problem, let it go. Stop wasting energy on it. That which you are willing to let go of will be solved. That does not mean that you do not try to work it out. Do not wear yourself out trying to resolve it. You do all you can, and if that does not work, then you say, "Okay, you take it, God. I have done all I can."

How many of you have used a Rubic cube? Have you ever solved it? When you put that cube down, you do not feel that it is going to end your life if you have not solved it. If something does not work out in life, it is not going to end your life. You are going to be able to go on to other things and come back to it when you are ready for it. A seven-year-old who wants to drive can come back to it at eighteen and drive. Very often there is a tendency to be so busy looking ahead that you try to do it too soon, and then you feel burdened by it. When there is a need for change, you will know it and feel it. How you handle it matters. If you bewail where you are and do nothing to take you out of that space, you will stay exactly where you are. But, if you look constructively at where you are and constructively at what you wish to have, you will be able to create that which will give you the change that you need. Remember, you have the power within you to bring that change about.

One of the most difficult areas in life is how to know when you must let go of something. You must first ask how valuable it is in your life. If you say it is very valuable, then ask what it has given you. If it has given you seven years of pain, then it is time to get rid of it. If it is blocking your ability to move on, you have outgrown it.

Some twenty-one-year-olds still want to sleep with a seven-year-old teddy bear. One might say that is foolish. Why? If that gives them a sense of comfort, that is fine. You must ask yourself if it still fits in your life at *this* point and time. Ask if it is still a valid reason for using your energy. If it is not a proper use of your energy, you begin the process of letting it go.

You have to ask how valid is it at this point in time in my life? How much right does it have to my energy? Where is it taking me? If it is taking you to destruction, if it is taking you to another seven years of misery, it is time for you to really look and decide. Remember that the only thing that is absolute in your world is change.

There are times when life is going to be different, your needs are going to be different, how you feel about things is going to be different, and what is most important to you is going to be different. Each time that occurs, you are going to have to ask yourself what you are holding on to. Have you ever looked in some of your drawers? There are things there that you cannot remember where they came from. You may have drawers full of all kinds of nuts, bolts, and screws which may be vital to something, but what? Periodically, go through and clean them out. Go through, bless it, give it to someone else and let it serve them. They may be ready for that item just as you may be ready to get rid of it.

You cannot move forward in the present while you are tying yourself to the past. That does not mean you do not have fond memories of the past. Every fond memory you have is in the head and the heart. If those thoughts from the past are not fond memories, why have them at all? Get rid of them. Bless them and let them go.

Do you realize the power you wield? How your facial expressions, the tone of your voice, or the words you choose can debilitate another or make them soar. It is a mighty power you have. Take time to be you, use your power to give others that which you would like to have. When you do that, you will be amazed at what comes back.

Most people have the feeling that pain in some way purges them. If they hurt enough, it is okay that they did it. You feel pain at certain times for another, or for some reason. That is a compassionate association. In a grieving situation, there is pain, as in loss by death, a divorce, a separation, or an ending of anything. A loss has a tearing. What has been together has separated, and there is a rending. There is pain and it needs to heal. It is wise to express the pain, but not to wallow in it. Say, "I hurt," and then do something constructive with that energy.

When you are overcome by feelings of despair or loneliness, look to its opposite polarity in order to overcome this feeling. Sometimes if you look at something with a sense of humor, you are able to put it into new perspective. If, for instance, you get a feeling of loneliness, do something. Call a friend and talk with them. Put an action in that place. Begin telling yourself that it is amazing how you do not get lonely anymore. Remember, there is a difference between being lonely and being alone. Time alone can be rewarding; do not confuse the two. The more you tell yourself that you are not alone, the sooner the subconscious begins to register it. The subconscious then releases it through the pituitary to the body, and you no longer feel it.

Every time you make a statement that says, "Every night . . . ." you are deeply impregnating the subconscious with that thought. That is the only thought that it is going to accept as fact and manifest. Change the thinking pattern, change the verbal expression, and get physical action going. You will find changes beginning to occur.

The first thing you should do whenever you want to change a situation is change how you think about it. Many people who think they are very positive are, in reality, very negative. If they would listen to themselves, if they were to tape their conversations and play them over, they would be shocked. Recognize that the power is within *you* to change you. This is done by changing how you view a situation and what your attitudes are toward the situation. By being willing to take a new view of the situation, you begin to move the energies to a new space which, in turn, permits new realizations to occur.

Doubt can be a very positive thing if it is leading you to suspect that something in your life is not good for you. "I am beginning to doubt that this is really good for me. Perhaps I should take another look." Doubt does not say, "I am not worthy." A doubt should direct you to take a second look. It may give you a second chance. Perhaps you will need a fifteenth chance. Always know that you are worthy of change. Many times, because of situations in the life, one has been led to a particular career. One decides that they will take up a certain profession because it has been in the family for years. Father was a lawyer, grandfather was a judge, so it seems logical that you become one yourself. Later, as the aggression periods let themselves be known, you begin to question the validity of your spending your life in that frame. You begin thinking about possible alternatives. Sometimes a person finds that they must work at something that has not been their heart's desire because the situation called for it. There are the wife and children, and they need to support them. They begin to feel trapped in the very thing that has been giving them support. At that point, there has to be a realization of a need for change. What you give to it is what you get. If every thought of that entrapment is one of negativity, then you are not going to be able to attract any positive change. Instead, you will probably attract a great deal of unhappiness to the situation. However, if you recognize that you are quite capable of change and this is a stepping stone in learning, you can move forward with it. You permit yourself to give it positive direction and when you give it that, good returns in the form of change. There is always the opportunity to change through participation. Change does not necessarily need to come from upheaval.

There is an association between aggression in the individual and aggression in the universe. They are tied together. Aggression in individuals will eventually become collective aggression. Have you ever noticed a pep rally? "Get out and kill them!" The fine and lovely team members on that day become killers. They have all joined their energies in order to win. In a warlike situation, there is an energy that becomes one and is focused on whatever that war is about. The power that can lead toward war can lead away from war. I will tell you that the prayer, power, and meditation that is being expended by the light groups all over the universe is effective. It is holding war in abeyance. Right now the energy of war is being held at bay. Keep it up! Do not stop seeing that it does not have to be. Every time you say it is inevitable, you are pounding another nail into whatever is being built.

Before you march "for peace;" make sure you are not hating anyone, or at war with yourself. If you are, your "vote for peace" does not count!

———————————————————————Julian

**If you have trouble
climbing the fence,
try opening the gate.**

—Julian

CHAPTER ★ VIII

Growth Through Soul-Development

Every single thing that you do in your life affects the soul and your growth. Any incident in the life can release emotional memories. If you cannot identify where it is coming from, it is time to re-examine the emotion. Time itself is needed to clarify why you feel a certain way. If nothing you have experienced in this life explains it, you can accept it as an emotional memory from the past. Take a moment to bless it and release it. Remember your thinking pattern creates the value of the incident. Permit yourself to redirect your energy to a new understanding. Once you think differently, you will act accordingly and reap the rewards of the new thought. It is then that the true conversion occurs. The law of cause and effect is always in motion and can never be stopped.

You are a human being with human emotions, and they will express themselves. There are going to be times when you have envy, anger, desire, or some negative emotions toward another. It is not the fact that they come, but what you do with them that matters. "I may get angry at you, but then, I have a choice. Either I let the ego take over and build it into something out of proportion, or I may say, 'Whoops, sorry about that,' and go on in a positive frame." Many times people get caught in the fact that they catch themselves in something negative.

When you catch yourself in a negative, reverse it by going to its polarity, a positive, but do not hold a guilt. Do not self-flagellate. You may say, "I blew it," but now it is already a new moment. When you ask the question, it is already the past. When you have a sense of negativity, it is the degree to which you build it that becomes the criterion of what it is doing to the soul. The same thing is true with picking up thoughts from the astral. You may pick up thoughts which are just horrendous, but you do not have to make them yours. You have the power and divine right of discernment. You must discern what you will make yours and what you will not.

The universal law of cause and effect is always in motion and can never be stopped and will take care of it all. You do not have to worry about getting even. There is nothing that escapes the universal law, so whenever you face someone negative, remember that you need not concern yourself with where they are going. Be concerned where *you* are going and that you are always a point of Light. The thing to remember is that if you are solid in yourself, if you have a realization of your own reality and a belief in it, nothing shall destroy it. You will continue to believe in yourself. If you believe in yourself, others will then have to begin to believe in you. Tell any person who is negative that they can stew in negativity if they choose, but that is not for you. Be yourself and remain cheerful.

In order to grow in soul, the real self must experience giving and taking; you have to experience all sorts of emotion. Man is a placid being, and he would not present a friction within which to grow. Therefore, others very often create the friction for him to cope with as a proof of his ability to overcome. The very negatives in life serve as a growth factor. In that manner, what appears to be a negative is in reality a positive providing an opportunity for growth. You grow from the pleasant times as well, but it is the interaction which provides the challenge for soul growth.

Circumstances do play a part in the life. During the early years, there are parental and environmental influences which greatly determine your direction. They are not necessarily negative. It is what you do with that direction that counts. You may have moved from one area to another, but you still have the opportunity to use your energies wherever you are. That which is happening in the life is also geared to the lessons which are necessary for your individual growth.

Whenever certain things are extremely repetitious in the life, they usually have reason for being there. It is a part of soul growth in some way. Look back at those incidents and your feelings about them and see how you felt. The older you get, the more you should logically believe that you can control your life. A sense of having control to a greater degree makes a difference about how you feel about the situation.

You are supposed to work out your own lessons. You do this through free will. God granted you free will, and He will not rescind the gift. Therefore, free will determines how you choose to work it out. For example, a person may choose to become a banker. He had within him all the potentials to become a businessman. He chose to use them in this specific field. Free will determined how he used his abilities. If your soul lesson is to learn a certain thing, you will learn that thing. How you learn it will be decided by free will.

In every life, that which was learned was imprinted to whatever degree you achieved it. For instance, you may have bits and pieces all gearing toward a totality of one particular thing. If there is an essence of patience to be learned, it may take many lifetimes to reach the degree of that quality which really gives you patience. In the earth plane, you deal with emotions which then present challenges and numerous opportunities to learn. In the spirit world you *understand* emotions, but emotion does not function. There are no feuding spirits in the hierarchy (in the high planes). You could stay in the spirit world forever, but you would not evolve as rapidly. A chance to move forward more rapidly by emotional interaction makes this physical plane a school.

You have one life. What you call a life is a chapter in the one soul's journey. You may be called by fifteen names in fifteen lives, but you are really one soul.

Your physical body is the temple, or the house, that the soul lives in and should be shown the exact same respect as the soul. There is no separation. If you mistreat your body, you are mistreating your soul in a sense. You are showing it disrespect.

What becomes of your physical body stems from your own consciousness. How you think about your body will determine what manifests in the body. If you respect your body, you will take care of it. That has nothing to do with whether you make your hair blond, red, white, or whatever. It has nothing to do with cosmetics you use or the colors you wear. That is personality-oriented, ego-oriented. The soul and the body respect each other, which means proper nourishment and proper care.

You enter earth with emotional memories. You are not consciously aware of them. A smell, an odor, or a piece of music will trigger an emotional memory in you. For instance, if you are experiencing a beautiful love and are surrounded by the smell of orange blossoms, then all of your life that odor may trigger a feeling of love. The same thing occurs with emotional traumas of a more negative nature. You feel it without understanding where it comes from, which can cause a real problem because you are feeling it without a means of identifying.

In every life experience, there are certain soul growth areas that you encounter, encompass, and hopefully achieve. When you are in my atmosphere, my side of the veil, you are in your totality. You are all that you have been in all things. You are everything the soul has collectively achieved. The personality factor dissipates when you leave because it was there to serve you in that particular life only. The love memory never dies. Experiences of the soul never die. In each round, or each chapter, in your sojourn, *you* determine how you want to grow. *Your* free will directs how you will grow. You come back by choice. Those experiences from the life are taken into the soul and will be retained in their totality in my world. Once free will was assigned, decisions were made, and those decisions brought action and responsibility.

Everything you have ever known was in the soul's consciousness when you came in. Everything that you have not known is in the universal consciousness because it is collectively what everyone has known. Beyond that is the "No Thing" which is the essence of all things. At any point in life you may use your awareness to tap those wells and drink freely, provided you are tapping them for mankind and for your own soul's growth. If you misuse them, you are impeding your growth. Every life you have ever lived is serving you now.

Through the many chapters of your life, you may elect to incarnate on one of several universes. There are many schools, or universes, and each one has its own lesson to teach. It does not matter where you learn or grow spiritually. Each plane has its own set of energies and emotions to be worked with.

When you decide to enter this world and have chosen your soul growth lesson and karmic pattern to work with, you will await the configuration of the heavens which will give you an energy packet, or signet, which will be your basic relationship to your soul in that life. This energy configuration gives you the opportunity to encounter, encompass, and react to the soul growth lessons you will face in life. This accounts for why some people will be quiet and others will not be, why some will feel a greater sense of creative flow and others will have a more structured direction. This energy is not personal. *you* personalize it. You create a personality during the specific lifetime, using or abusing it as you choose.

Karma is associated with growth, because as you work through karma, you expand the soul's comprehension. Karma does not have to be "an eye for an eye." There is no incident in your life that is not related to karma or the creation of it. If you are not cleaning it up, you are making it—good or bad. The degree to which karma is created depends on the incident. You must live your life in a manner that is loving. Do not worry about your past karma, but pay attention to what you might be creating. As you begin to live that way, you will automatically find the means of cleaning up the past. The soul knows what you came in to clean up and *you* create the rest.

You have to always remember that no one knows when karma is involved. That is one of the reasons why reincarnation has been very hard for some people to comprehend or accept. Anything wrong was blamed on karma. The cat died and it was karma. Your attitude in life is very often manifested in your body. Thus, all illness is not karmic. Remember that you are dealing with many things that have evolved. You are dealing with genetics.

You are dealing with a very complicated system of bone, muscle, tendon, and cell. Each of them has an ability to cooperate with the other when held in respect and taken care of. You have to recognize that there are many things that influence every situation.

A soul may incarnate in a body which is born deformed or handicapped. It can be that this situation was predetermined. It can be that the determination was that the genetic process within the body would present the necessary condition. There is no way for anybody to know. That is why you must assume that the thing you do with any situation is to make the best of it. You do the best you can with what you have at any point in time.

You are given everything you have to use, and it is right and proper that you do use it. You each evolve at your own rate. You cannot fail. There are no flunkies. There is no soul ever lost. You may be a little slow and tag along, but you are never lost. You are always worked with. God has infinite patience and never gives up.

You can and have gone to many solar systems in your path of evolving. They seem new to you because earth is where you are supposed to be working now. They each afford you the opportunity for another growth factor.

The soul, or the immortal part of yourself, takes a raw energy around it which is like a cocoon. You develop this as a personality structure. When you leave the earth plane, that gradually dissolves and you are your totality. This totality is the reality of your collective lives. The soul is imprinted with the lessons and experiences of that life, but not the personality. The soul goes back to its state of totality having gained from that life what it had to gain.

The only reason for knowing about a past life is for its influence to assist in this life in some way. For instance, in this life, if you are female, those lives prior as a female may have been a major influence in relationship to this life. It does not matter what you have been in the past; it matters what kind of life you led. It is an emotional memory that affects this life and triggers changes in this life from past lives. If your particular role in this life deals with things of a past life, they will be the ones that you are told about. You are not necessarily here to repeat that life. Everyone has been both sexes.

Your goal in life should be to arrive at a state of humbleness, a state where there is no separation. The higher the elevation, the less the separation. The less need there is for ego, prestige, and position. The person who tells you they are too highly evolved to mingle with somebody has not made it over the curve yet. There are no privileges to the evolved. The evolved walk among those who are not evolved in love. In the hierarchy, there are no pecking orders. There is no good, better, best. There is only assignment. The higher you are, the less separation there is from anyone, and the less need there is for special treatment.

Those who have reached the high consciousness, where they do not need to return, may still choose to do so. Some people, who have already reached that plateau, choose to come back in service to others. You will never know it. They will never get up and announce it, for they are beyond ego.

**Humbleness
is not subservience;
it is acceptance.**
——————————————Julian

Night is but the pause
before a new dawn.
The dark times of life—
but the pause before
a new illumination.
In both cases, one waits
with certainty that
the light will come.

———————————————Julian

CHAPTER ★ IX

The Final Growth: Transformation

Death is a dignity. It is a transition from one phase of yourself to another and should·be treated as a dignity, not as something you try to hide. I have a perfect example in a young child who was close to a relative dying from cancer. The child was told in an unemotional way that this relative was dying from cancer. On the day when his relative was close to death, this lad was called to the bedside. After exchanging a few words with the dying man, he was told to go out and play. The marvelous thing about this man was that he let the child see his position in the beginning. He showed him the bumps and he was able to see that there was something there. When he said, "I am going to die, but you go out and play," he gave the child a normality to replace the seeming abnormality of death. He understood the child might not comprehend his death. He set in motion for the child a fine and beautiful thing. The fact that there was an open exchange and respect helped the child overcome the difficulty associated with an incident of this nature.

Parents or adults at a time of transition (death) often try to shield the child from something they think the child cannot handle. They are thinking that the child is functioning on the same level of energy as they are. The child, according to the closeness of the person who has made the transition, is going to feel the loss. He is going to ask why they are not here. Unless at that time, death (as you call it) is treated as a normal thing, the child can begin to build fears of losing everyone. In most cases, if you have not seen the final curtain of a person's transition, you may have trouble accepting that they are gone, whether you are an adult or a child.

One of the hardest acceptances is during wartime when notification of death arrives. They never see the body. A child should be permitted the choice of remembering grandpa or grandma as they were the last time they saw them, or in their final state. Always recognize that this is part of another cycle. People should realize that children need an explanation, not a fantasy or a fairy tale, because they have much more stamina than you think. Do not tell a child that the deceased is sleeping. This could lead to associating sleep with death and being gone and could create a fear of sleep.

Physical death in this world is predetermined to a degree. It is predetermined by a specific collection of events. It is sometimes thrown out of focus, but not to the degree that you go before your time. Many times a person will face what appears to be death. You learn from these experiences as they were a part of your soul growth. If any one of them had been meant to be your final day, you would have gone. Please remember that how you think affects how things affect you.

Upon death or the passing from this plane a sleep state is entered. This is to permit a detachment and acceptance of where the soul is. An adjustment is made to the Light body. After that there is a gradual lessening of the personality state. They might no longer care about the pet name or who got their favorite ring. Love, however, does not die.

People who commit suicide have made a free will choice to end something. Some suicides are a karmic thing that must be experienced. For these people, it is truly the proper time. Others have made a freewill choice. Those persons will have to face that which they have not faced, or were unable to face, at another time. In the interim, the soul will be worked with, taught, assisted in every way to bring it to its full strength and realization. This will give them, in the future, a more distinct probability that they will not make the same choice. No soul is ever lost.

It is very important for you to realize that none of you are the worst and none of you are the best, but each a delightful human being with a little of both, for the polarity must be there. When I look at the world, I see hidden within many very organized, dutiful people a great desire to, just once, kick over the traces and do something utterly ridiculous. There is, in everyone who appears to have no direction whatsoever, an inner desire to, just once, have it all together, if only for one day. That is polarity speaking.

Through the will, one shapes and molds their life from beginning to end and to new beginnings again. Life is a cycle, and you direct its flow. When the soul has rested, it decides on its next journey and the next series of lessons. Once again, that new born babe will be shaped and molded to self-discovery. How wonderful! Believe and understand that the gift of free will and spiritual guidance is never lost. You are all divine beings with potential and ability. You will learn to tap these energies, use these energies, and share these energies. How wonderful life is!

As we end this chapter, the most important questions you can ask yourself is, "What am I doing today?"

"What am I doing right now!" If you will take each day and live it to its fullest with the positive thought of progression in it, you will grow. This means you are doing the best you can with what you have; you are not bewailing what you do not have. You will find yourself growing and coming to a new understanding of yourself. If you meditate or are someone who works with prayer, you are going to be bringing into focus the inner self which will help you all the way. Do it! You have it! It *is* in there! Do not be afraid to listen to *you*. When you are listening to you in that sense, you are listening to the God-self, to the self that is not ego-bound. Please remember the new age commandment: *Love one another unconditionally.* Remember, what you send out returns to you!

Do not be afraid of change; reruns become boring after a while.

——— —Julian

THE DIVINITY PRAYER

There is a divinity within me
that no man can destroy.

There is a Light within me
that only I can dim.

As I focus upon this Light;
it is my perfection,
my protection,
my very being.

It wells within me and fills me
It surrounds me and protects me.

It releases me from all negativity
and permits my self to move forward
in certainty that wholeness and
Light are mine, and no thing or
being can destroy it.

For the Father and I are one,
and cannot be separated.

I know this with a certainty.

I feel it and experience it.

God is, I am; and we are one.

—Julian

Put your energy into seeking solutions— not creating delusions.

—Julian

CHAPTER ★ X

Understanding Manifestation

"Self-Discovery" was absolutely necessary before exposure to the energies in this material. You had to first have an opportunity to bring balance to yourself before you could begin to elevate the energies that are associated with manifestation.

Manifestation energies, whether you realize it or not, result from every thought you have—good, bad, or indifferent. Thoughts have a manifestation quality in your life, thus, creating an energy to which you must respond. Even a fleeting thought can bring a change in the energy surrounding you which permits good or bad (depending on how you look at it) to come into the life.

Please understand that manifestation is not a parlor trick. It is hard dedication to the self and, through that self-dedication, dedication to the God-self. It is not ego-ridden. It is saying that you accept the God in you, and together you manifest. If you think to use manifestation toward another for a negative purpose, be very careful. Energy which you send out can only return to its source—you. It is like a boomerang. If you manifest ill toward another, the only place it is going to come to roost is in you; therefore, you must be willing to use this energy wisely.

Manifestation or transition energies are not energies

that can be taken flippantly or lightly. They are not energies with which you play; they are energies with which you work. They are there to manifest changes in the life—changes within your body, changes within your consciousness and your ability to rise with that consciousness to a greater sense of your own potential.

One of the first things you must realize is that you and you alone, individually, are responsible for what happens to you. You and you alone are the control factor for how the energies will be used by you with this material. How much you accomplish will be determined by how much you permit yourself to flow with the material and how much you work with it on your own.

People take many courses relating to consciousness levels, and each works with some level of consciousness elevation. Thus, everybody has a different interpretation of what consciousness means. They have a feeling that this is something reserved for a time of meditation or during a time of a class. Most people do not see it as something to be lived with. The responsibility for where that consciousness takes you rests with the individual. It is the individual who prepares the focus from which his manifestation occurs. The important realization must be that the manifestation focus must be lived on *all* levels of the existence, not just in thought-form. Therefore, one cannot try to manifest a peaceful work situation while being argumentative and hostile at home. As you read these chapters, you must recognize that putting it into practice will take time and effort on your part. Just reading is not enough. You cannot say you are going to go into this divine place and have this special experience while hating your neighbor. You must make some decisions along the way about how you are going to live the understanding you have gained. You are going to let that energy flow through you every moment of your life, not just for one hour in a specific class. That is where most people make their mistake in dealing with transition energies. They have the feeling that it is something you use only when trying to manifest something in your life, or while attending a class, but they do not see it as something to be lived.

In "Self-Discovery," we went through some of the natural, normal feelings that you go through during the seven-year cycles and in the growing pattern in the elevation of yourself. You were given some suggestions to help you with those feelings. If you have worked with them, you will have brought into your life a new sense of balance and discovery. For some, it may seem as if negative things are happening. It may seem that everything you thought was going just the way you wanted, suddenly is not. You must realize that manifestation energy is an energy that brings you realization and comprehension on another level, that helps you make decisions, not based on A relating to B, B to C, C to D; but how to get from A to E. It is not always logical. Your initial thought-form was based on preconceived ideas, that which you already knew. Your logic told you it would probably manifest in a certain way. The manifestation energy is beyond the boundaries of preconceived logic. It manifests in the *best* way. You may find it confusing when it does not seem to be occurring *your* way, but if you are patient, you will see that it *is* manifesting.

You are going to begin building a recognition of these energies. Some of the things we talk about here may seem a little strange—not strange "hocus-pocus," but strange because they do not seem to have a relationship to transition energies at the point where you are looking at them.

You may rest assured that anything that is presented here has an absolute relationship to your being able to use your *own* energies to transform your life. There is not one person reading this material who does not have a greater potential than he has realized, admitted to, or expressed. As you work with these transition energies, you are going to find parts of yourself becoming clearer and clearer to you. You will better be able to work with them with the techniques you will learn.

Let us look at ritual. What part does ritual play in any transition of energy? Ritual is doing the same thing in the same way for the same purpose each time. Any use of a specific affirmation to enter a specific state of consciousness is a ritual. It is a ritual because it is the same every time. The sameness brings with it a comfort and security which permits trust. Any time that you repeatedly do the same thing in the exact same way, you are creating a ritual and a space in which you feel secure.

Symbolism has been a part of ritual from the beginning of time. Light represents the high consciousness, and light in the form of candles has been used from early times as a point of consciousness. When you light the candle, what are you doing? You are dispersing darkness; you are expressing the desire to see, not outwardly, necessarily, but inwardly. As dogmatic practices and philosophic expressions developed, ritual became a living part of them. It became an outward expression through symbolization.

When a group of people do the same thing at the same time, there is a unison of action which creates a rapport among everyone taking part. When you are asked to participate in a single sound, there is a union through that sound. This explains why groups of people come together with the same interests; they come together to participate in a ritual of sameness. The rituals that you hear about, no matter what they are being used for, have the same purpose, to bring into unity, into oneness, those who are participating in it.

I would like you to repeat and use this statement:

"I am, God is, and we are one."

Say it three times. Can you feel the difference in a repetitious statement? The energy grows through repetition. It becomes a new coordinate of power. Every time you repeat something, it is not only convincing the subconscious that it is so, but it is altering the energies around you. It is permitting those energies to elevate. It does not matter what you call God, but it does matter that you call upon Him. It does not matter what name you have used through time, it does matter that you recognize that His energy force and you are one. His divine force lifts you above the mundane and shows you clear direction.

I would like you to repeat and use this statement:

"I am worthy!"

Repeat it three times. Do you understand what is happening to you? You are suddenly beginning to tune to a vibration that says, "Maybe I am. Maybe I am not the poor slob I thought I was." When one does not find themselves in the space they desire to be in, one of two things occurs, the removal of self-responsibility which puts the blame on everyone else or self-flagellation which says "I am not worthy." Neither is the answer to the problem. Instead, one must be willing to question what might be changed in attitude to let the manifestation occur.

One of the things to understand during this study is that what you think of yourself results in what is brought to you. If you are afraid of falling, you are going to fall.

You are going to be so afraid of falling that you are going to manifest all sorts of clumsy actions until you fall. It will not be because you had to fall, or because you are supposed to fall. It will be because your own thinking pattern has manifested the ability to fall—"that which you fear . . . "

Always remember, for any divine action to occur, it must be supported by physical action in the physical world. The person who constantly says he would like to go to the theater, but never calls to find out about tickets will probably never get to the theater. If he makes the call to inquire about tickets, he will be putting into action all kinds of energy in relationship to theater. He may go to the theater as someone's guest, or he may end up working there. Any number of things can happen. The physical act of reaching toward the goal you wish to accomplish will put the energy into motion.

The first step to overcoming fears of failure is the acceptance of the fact that you can. Failure, in reality, does not exist. That which does not work is pushing you toward that which will work. In your world, basketball requires tall people. If you are three feet tall and your desire is to become a basketball player, very logically, you will not. That is not a failure. It is because you were not meant to be. Many times, in trying to manifest something in your life, you manifest *illusions* rather than reality. Where those illusions come from is very often determined by other people's opinions, or something that you have identified in life as success.

What represents success to you? To some, it is a large bank account; to others, it is a large car; still others think it is a perfect spouse. People interpret success differently. If it is a large bank account that you want, it means that a responsibility to manifest it begins with you. How do you manifest it? If you are going to have a large bank account, you will want a large income. It probably calls for a skill, and that skill probably calls for schooling, and that schooling probably calls for dedication and application of your energy. In your world you call it discipline. If you do not give it that energy, you are not going to be able to manifest it—unless you take another route, which might be to take the fruits of other people's work. In other words, they earn it; you steal it.

There is just as much energy put into stealing something as there is into earning it, but with a big difference in how you feel at the end. If you have worked and earned, you have a sense of oneness with it. If you have not, you have a momentary feeling of elation. "Ah-ha! I did it! I put it over!" Then you live with it, and living with it becomes a thorn in the side. There is a moral issue that comes into being. Maybe you did not ask for it, but because you are an emotional being, it is there.

This may sound like so much chatter, but what we are doing is beginning to focus on the responsibility of manifestation. You can manifest anything you want in your life, but you may not feel fulfilled by it. If what you manifest is not related to the soul, the fulfillment will not be there. If it is only related to ego and personality, it can not possibly bring you fulfillment, no matter how great it is. That does not mean that you do not have a right to have monetary return for services rendered. I ask: What do you want in your life? What is it you would really like to have?

You develop very often with more than one potential in life, and the direction of your focus may change. Recognize that each of them is a part of you, and at various points in the life, each serves you. You have to manifest the potential. Your desire may be to dance. You make an effort and put work into it and you dance. Later, your efforts may be directed to teach dance. You will then have the fulfillment on both levels of that potential. The potential of what you want to manifest as you go along may change, but you will be manifesting your potential from within yourself.

To be successful in manifestation, you must develop a focus, which means to limit the direction of your energies. Remember, if you are trying to focus on ten things, you are going to have a diminished focus and may have ten things happen haphazardly in your life. If you direct the energy to a single thing, you will then manifest that thing. Nothing precludes you from using the rest of your potential. For instance, if you choose to make dance your career, it does not mean you cannot do something in art as a hobby. The energy must be focused in a single place to make it a reality. That is why you focus on one thing first; then the potential of the peripheral comes into vision enough for you to begin to manifest them.

To focus on having a love relationship, one must first focus on loving. What is loving? Loving is sharing. Many times, one gets caught up in the projected stereotype fantasy of a love relationship—the knight in shining armor on the white horse, or the long hair coming out of the tower—fantasies that have come down through time. You have to really understand what love is, what you want out of love as well as what you are willing to give in love. Only when you have a clear understanding of these things can you manifest love.

Most people who go around saying nobody loves them are not very lovable people. They are full of hate, full of venom, full of resentment, and asking, "Why doesn't someone love me?" You cannot manifest that kind of negative energy in one part of yourself and expect sweetness and love to be attracted to you. You have to ask yourself how lovable *you* are? What is your attitude in relationship to love on all levels of your life, not just a particular personal emotion on a one-to-one basis? You must know what it is you really want, and then know that is what you are going to manifest.

Most manifestations fail because of vague imagery, an inability to transform a specific value because it is so vague. It could be anything. I have heard people in your world say, "Well, he is not the best in the world. He drinks, he doesn't work, he gambles—but he's there." Being there does not seem to be a very logical reason for having a love relationship with this person. You are really saying that you feel you must accept less. Time and time again, you set limitations on what you will accept in your life because you think that is all you can have. You cannot do that. You have to say, "In my life I will manifest," and realize that in that manifestation you have to feed every phase of its development. You cannot hate on the one side and expect all good to come to you on the other. Across the board in your life, you must begin to manifest the kind of things *in you* that you want to attract *to you.*

In manifestation, confusion often arises between focus and flexibility. You must first focus upon a goal for manifestation. Secondly, you must have the flexibility within the range of your focus. If you want a specific type of job, you have to be flexible enough to go where those jobs are. It may mean that those types of jobs are not close by. The focus is the type of job, where you work is the flexibility. The ability being focused does not take away from the fact that you will have to accept the job from wherever it comes.

Focus is necessary. Know what you want by quality,

but also leave room for flexibility. For instance, there are many people who are meant to serve in one capacity in life and spend all their time trying to manifest something else. It is usually based on admiring what someone else has achieved. "I want to be a teacher; I always wanted to teach, and here I am an ophthalmologist." Look at the service that is being given!

A potential will manifest, but the avenue through which it manifests is the flexibility. When you want a specific kind of job, ask yourself if that is the job on which your energies can really focus happily. Why do I want it? If you are not sure that it is to your highest good, you ask that within your ability you see more of your potential. You cannot say you do not know what you want to do, because if you do not know what you want to do, you have nothing in which to put energy. Pick something and put energy into it.

There is danger in letting the ego-personality rule the focus. You have to have the soul tied to the purpose. If fulfillment of the soul is part of the focus, then it is fine. If you are focusing a relationship and if you are focusing on all the surface things instead of the qualities, you can block a perfect potential from coming to you. If there is someone without those surface specifics available who can give you everything else, you have blocked it by that description. Focus on the quality, not the personality.

There are times when things will manifest without any focus or directed attention from the conscious mind. This is because the inner self triggers the potential. When the ability and potential are there, the inner self knows it is time for that door to be opened, even though the conscious ego-self is not feeling the need. The inner self triggers the potential. It is said that, when the student is ready, the teacher appears. "As a man thinks in the heart, so shall it be brought unto him." You may be saying one thing with your mouth and another in your heart. That which is in your heart is going to manifest.

If you have an equal interest in several things, and you cannot choose one over the other, take one of them and put the energy and focus into it. Let the others fall on the periphery. If you do not feel what you have chosen is to your liking, there is nothing to say that you cannot go into one of the others. You can spend your whole life trying to decide, whereas, if you choose one, you have one with which to work.

Please understand that people often give the name of God and soul to something to make it legal. "I want to win the lottery because then I can do a lot of good for a lot of people." How about getting a job, working at it and getting money to help a lot of people? A lottery means a lot of money coming to you at once. You have not had to put anything out for it—except the buying of a ticket, which is not too much effort. The point is you have to put effort and energy into a manifestation. You have to treat it as if it is already yours, as if it is your absolute right to have it. Then it manifests.

I shall spend a little time with relationships because it is a very important part of people's lives. Very often a person waits, wanting a relationship, but it does not manifest. If they are looking to the relationship to answer their needs and to make them whole, they are not ready for the relationship. They have never looked into their willingness to share or give. A relationship is a sharing. Through self-discovery, one becomes whole and may then choose to share that wholeness. The responsibility for happiness cannot be placed outside the self.

If you have a need for love, you will attract to you various love energies. If you have not been specific about that energy, how that energy will serve you will be non-specific. You may have a lot of loves come into the life that do not have the ingredients you want. It is not selfish to figure out what you want in your life as long as you are seeing your responsibilities to it. Nebulous statements buy nebulous results.

Many times, people want a mate because everybody else has one, and it seems like the right thing to do. Deep inside, however, they are not sure they want that commitment. There is nothing wrong with choosing to be a whole individual by yourself. Be sure that what you are feeling is not the result of what others say, that you are not saying or feeling it because you think you are supposed to. That is never going to work. It only works when it is something you really feel within yourself.

In your world today, there is a big drive for women's rights. You are finding, more and more, an equalization in the sharing of life between male and female because of the cultural changes. This is saying that the old roles—man works and woman takes care of the house and has children—no longer apply. It may be that the man thoroughly enjoys staying home, taking care of children, and doing things around the home, and the woman has the drive to have a career. There is nothing wrong with that as long as it is right for both of them.

The stereotypes, the traditions created in your world, are beginning to have their foundations shaken, and there are a lot of questions that come up in relationships. You must always look at yourself and see what is happening to you. If the same pattern happens over and over again where relationships are concerned, then the change must take place in *you*. If you are attracting the same thing over and over again, you must look at yourself and have a personal reevaluation to find out why you are repeating the same thing again and again, indicating that you have not discovered what the lesson was. If you are repeating a pattern, take time to look at yourself. You will find out that by changing the inner self, you may perhaps change your whole life.

I have seen instances in your world where one is enamored of another, and the whole life has been destroyed because that feeling was not reciprocated, even though that person did not rightfully belong to them. That is not love, that is ego. A person enamored of another who has not had their feelings reciprocated must make a choice. Perhaps that person was not meant to be theirs. They can choose to destroy their life by refusing to let go, or recognize their love belongs somewhere else. Recognize that in your world, there is more than one person who is right and perfect for you to love. Most people think there is only one person in the whole world for them. It is very nice if the first one you find is the one you want to be with, but if it does not work out with that person, do not think there will not be someone else.

Man makes excuses for what he thinks of as failures. If a relationship does not work, it is very obvious it would not have worked as a permanent situation. If you had really succeeded in a relationship with that person, you probably would not have been a bit happier. Chalk one up to experience. Take a look at the situation and make a decision. "Do I really want to put all my energy into that, or do I want to put that energy into me and my own growth, into my own experience?" There are as many variables in relationships as there are in manifestation. It is because every energy is individual. Always ask yourself if you are coming out on the short end of the stick. If you are, then it is time to look elsewhere.

If you look elsewhere, please be sure it is after really

examining yourself. Do not go off in a huff. In the world today, manifestation of many unhappy relationships is occurring, and it is because of the attitudes being used in the entry into those relationships. There was a time in your world when a relationship was entered into with the sole thought that the relationship would last and be strong and loving. That thought held through the ups and downs in the life. Today relationships are entered into with the thought that, if it does not work, we can always end it. How can anything succeed when it is based on that foundation? You are already defeating it before you get into it.

People look around and say, "Well, that is the way the world is today." The world is the way it is today because of the thinking-patterns and manifestations of those thinking-patterns. A relationship is a giving and taking. The giving you might enjoy; some of the taking you might not. Usually, if you have to worry about whether you should stay with it or not, it is an indication that there is something vitally wrong. Either you or the other person must make a change within the self. A change of perspective can usually restore the balance.

Look within yourself. You can cast mud and complain about how terrible the other person is, but ask yourself what you have done in this relationship, to this relationship. The only one you can change is you, you cannot change anyone else. You have to ask yourself if you are willing to put up with it.

I have heard people in your world say, "I've stayed with this bum for twenty years, and for twenty years he has been nothing but misery to me." And someone asks, "Why don't you leave?" The answer is, "I couldn't do that!" Love and value yourself, not through the ego, but through the soul. When you do that, you will attract that to you which is much more fulfilling, and it will be much better.

Loving the self means, even when I falter, I'm okay, because at least I know I faltered. It is the acceptance of yourself, not as you dream or think you should be, but as you are.

Hearing is the first sense to come and the last to go—and one of the senses the least used in between. Be still and listen, not to what you chatter with the mouth, but to what is going on in the depths of you. As you are quiet with yourself, you get in touch with the superconscious self, which helps you to see your value, and you will begin to feel at ease with yourself. When you are constantly dissatisfied with yourself, you are really saying you are not good enough, that you need to be something more in order to be acceptable.

It is natural to care about what others think about something, but it cannot be permitted to get out of hand. Opinions are exchanged and ideas expressed, but ultimately, you, and only you, must decide what is right for you. After all, you will be responsible for that decision, so why should it be someone else's? Discussion helps you to see all sides of something, but the end result must be from you. Don't be afraid to hear other people's opinions, but realize that if they differ from yours, it does not necessarily mean you are at fault. Only you can put you down. Evaluate, consider, and then decide for yourself. If I could give you one magic formula, it would be to spend time alone with yourself daily—no television, no phonograph, no tape, nothing but you. At first, it may seem like a contest of wills; because immediately, you are going to think of ten thousand things you should do. Know that it is legal to spend some time with yourself. It is all right, and from that will come an inner sense of peace which can show you what it is you need and want, because that superconscious mind knows exactly what your potential is. Do not give up on you!

Many times, one finds themselves thinking thoughts they know they should not be thinking. Everybody has thoughts that come to them unbidden. They come from things that you have heard or seen. When those thoughts come in, what you do is say: *I do not accept that as my thought. I do not accept that thought as my thought.* Then you are not making it one with you. Then think a happy thought instead.

Many times there are areas of yourself that you are not happy with and you know that there needs to be a change or improvement for you to be truly happy. You have to ask yourself the value of what you want to do and how much of your energy it is worth. Energy must be expended well. If you kicked the cat in anger, you can choose to spend four days bewailing that and really build it into a mammoth thing, or you can love the cat, ask its forgiveness, and release your anger through some positive action. That is energy well spent, the other is not. Question what made you angry in the first place.

You have to ask yourself why you determine something is not right. Many people see things in themselves as terrible because they see things out of focus. Always ask yourself how much energy it is worth and if it really matters. Because humbleness has been taught, you do not magnify the good, you magnify the bad. You take the "poor sinner" route as a natural reaction. As long as you are emphasizing the negatives in yourself, you are giving them a stronger foothold. Ask yourself if it really matters that you do something in a certain way.

If you have an ulcer and you are thinking constantly about the ulcer, the only thing you are giving energy to is the ulcer. If you think the opposite of ulcer, if you think wholeness, you are going to begin to heal the ulcer. Then take it to the cause of the ulcer. If you are looking for wholeness, if you ask for wholeness, and if you think wholeness, solving the problem has to occur within you because wholeness is part of it.

People go to a healer and ask him to heal their ulcer, and the healer does the healing. The following week, they will have something else disturb them because the cause has not been touched. If wholeness of the system is the goal, whatever is causing the problem has to come into focus within the realm of that healing. That is why the first things experienced in a healing are emotional; the change in the emotional attitude of the person begins the healing process.

If there are several aspects of your life with which you want to work in terms of manifestation, take one at a time. Otherwise you are taking the same amount of energy and dividing it into three places. If you have one cup of water and you divide it into three thimbles, that is the only amount of energy you can give to it. You have reduced the amount concentrated in one place to one-third the original capacity. You put the energy into one thing, bringing it into manifestation in the life and then go after another. Set your priorities. You can work on more than one at a time, of course, but they will take longer because you are dissipating the energy.

If you want to have your creative self expressed, you have to give it focus. You focus on creativity and doors to creativity open. If you "miss the boat" on the first opportunity, that is alright. Another will come as long as you are still focusing on the creative force.

Do not confuse self-satisfaction from the ego level with self-satisfaction on the soul level. I am talking about self-satisfaction from the soul level. Accepting yourself as you are at the soul level permits you to recognize the need for change. If you say to yourself, "I can accept the fact that I am not the greatest person in the world, I can accept that I use language that I should not use," that recognition is an improvement, because now you can do something about it. If your acceptance is in the ego sense, you will say it is all right for you to use any kind of language you want. That is not self-acceptance, that is self-excusing. When you are accepting yourself, always remember that you are approaching it from the soul level, not from ego. Therein lies the difference. The ego may set the goal. You have to have ego to have ambition and to have incentive. It becomes the focus, and everything related to that focus then has a relationship to it, but it has to come from the soul level too. It cannot be, "I want it because I want it." You have to know why you want it.

From work comes fulfillment, fulfillment that is from activation of the self. That fulfillment is not ego, that is soul. The ego says, "Look what I did." The soul says, "I feel so good about what I did." Therein lies the difference. If you take a moment to think about it, you will always know which is working.

In establishing study groups, if the purpose of the group is to have the teacher prominent before people, then it is not a spiritual idea. If the purpose is to share that which you have experienced or know, the desire to serve through that, then it is. Anything that you do to spread the spiritual practices can only be good to the extent that you practice them. You can read ten thousand books and mouth off from them, but unless you are living it, you are not a teacher of it. In other words, "Practice what you preach."

The purpose of this material is to teach you the techniques of manifestation that you may use it in all areas of the life. The very purpose of coming together with the *I Am* statement—*God and I are one*—has already manifested something. You are in His Light for the purpose of improving your ability to improve your own life, which is of great service to Him.

I would like you to begin working with several statements. These are the statements that you will use when you are working with manifestation:

> Infinite Spirit, fill me and surround me.
> Know that I release all negativity.
> I become an energy of pure Light
> that I may bring pure Light.

As you repeat this two or three times, it begins to build in you the realization that you are opening and releasing, and that you are accepting pure Light, that you are going to become pure Light, which means that you are going to be manifesting in Light. This means you will have the illumination which permits you to see and accept.

Think for a moment of what it is you would like to see manifested in your life. Now, ask yourself why. Begin to give it shape and form to the best of your ability. If you wish to manifest someone with whom you can share life, think in terms of the qualities you want. Think about it until it is no longer a nebulous thing, but something very real. If you are trying to see health, think of yourself at your very healthiest moment in life. See yourself when you were very healthy and remember it. That feeling is the focus of your life now. If it is security you are trying to manifest, think of a time in your life when you felt absolutely secure. Maybe it was a time when you did not yet understand security. You felt loved and protected by your parents. You did not know there were times of financial stress that existed in the world. Think of that secure feeling, because that is what you want to manifest in relationship to financial or emotional security. You take the essence of whatever it is, and you build with it. It is as if someone gave you clay and permitted you to start to shape and mold and build.

When you have achieved the focus, I want you to see Light surrounding it, lighting it and letting it grow, whether it is that feeling of health, that feeling of being loved—whatever it was—see it in Light. Is it not beautiful?

Now I want you to pick that up, literally, Light and all, and I want you to bring it to your brow, let yourself feel it. Now repeat these words:

> **My eyes are opened,**
> **I clearly see**
> **this perfect thought**
> **in relationship to me.**

And now, be quiet with it, seeing that Lighted vision directly in front of the third eye (your brow), focusing in you, focused by you.

At this point, if you can still accept it as what you really want, simply say:

> **I accept it.**
> **From this moment,**
> **it is a living part of me.**
> **So be it.**

I want to talk a little bit about sadness and joy and the feeling of release. Whenever you release anything, whether it is the most negative thing in your life or a positive thing, there is a sadness that goes with it because it is based on sacrifice, a letting go. Please remember that sacrifice is not blood on the altar, but a release, a letting go, an acceptance that it is all right to do so. The feeling of sadness and release are definitely related, but it is not a pain, but a melancholy sort of sadness. A habit long held and then released may leave you feeling as if something is missing. That is, the habit is missing and, in a sense, is being mourned for. You can now use your energy to create something new in your life.

Remember you made yourself light, you made yourself an instrument of light. You focused, you thought about it, you surrounded it with light, and you brought it to the third eye on the brow of comprehension on the highest plane and again identified with it there, then you accepted it. You made it a living part of you after really scrutinizing it.

When the energies of inner power are released, as when you are experiencing this, there is some tension, because you do not know what is going to happen. I want you to work with this every day, but not with a different thing each day. Stay with one thing for a week. Take a little time with this and really give it some scrutiny.

Always have those mental scales that ask, do I really want it, and always remember that there are no half-packages. If you want it, you will get the whole thing. If you want the baby, you will get the diapers. That is why you ask yourself "why?" do you really want that and all that goes with it?

You must exert discipline in working with this, and that is why I want you to work with it every day. Anything that is worth having takes time to have, and you have to work with it daily.

The sacrifice is the release of anything that stands in the way. It is necessary to give up something in order to get something. We have talked about sacrificing child-hood to become an adult. That means you must give up the temper tantrums of the childhood. You must realize that you cannot have both. When you say I release, it does not mean that you have to give up yourself, but it means you must be willing to let go of those things that are blocking what you want to manifest.

You cannot serve another unless you serve yourself. You can only give what you represent. The old teachings of humility say, "I am not worthy, I am not worthy." But you *are* worthy. You are worthy of the greatest potential you have. If you refuse to give attention to it to bring it into manifestation, you are denying the God within you.

Through service to self, you are able to serve others. For instance, a person who gives all his life and never provides for himself later in life bewails the fact that he has nothing. He created the situation by ignoring him-self. Service to others does not mean selflessness. It does not mean you do not help, or serve others, but you give the same dignity to the God *within you* as you are giving to the God within them. Through the ability to make your life better, you are able to make the lives of others better, so the service to self is the initiation to service.

A person who spends his whole life giving to others, totally believing that he will be taken care of himself, will also have to recognize that he must accept that care what-ever way it comes. People who think, "If I'm good to everybody else, everybody else is going to be good to me," give with a string attached. When you give with the understanding and realization that you will be taken care of, it will be so, because that is what you are manifesting. You are great manipulators in your world. Remember that you assist the manifestation by common sense physi-cal action toward it.

You must recognize the balance and polarity of giving. Giving can become destructive if you give too much and take away from another the ability to give. For instance, the child who is given everything and feels that is the way it is supposed to be and who does not feel any need to give even respect to another, has been destroyed by giving. At a point in giving, you have to take time to be the recipient, because the balance says the giver must also be the receiver, or he denies the gift of giving to another. You must keep the polarity. That is really part of this giving to the self, the recognition that it is all right for you to be a receiver too. When another has reached the point where they cannot understand the giving, you must bless them, leave it alone and withdraw until they are ready to understand more. They must be willing to receive in order for the gift to be of value, whether it is love, respect, or a material gift.

When you sit down to do this manifestation exercise daily, you are going to:

1. Use the opening statement.
2. Think about what it is you want.
3. Ask yourself why you want it.
4. Bring it into focus.
5. Surround it by the Light that you are.
6. Bring it to the brow for greater comprehension.
7. Accept it as rightfully yours.

Know from this minute on that everything you do is going to have some kind of relationship to what you decide to work at manifesting. You can word it anyway you wish. The thing is to have the thought that you are going to make it and that you are able to see it now in relation to you. If it is a dancer you want to be, you are going to see the hard work that goes with it, not the fantasy that is associated with it. You are going to see everything that goes with it.

Remember a time when you felt you had it all together. Remember a time when you felt whole. Relive that energy. Bring forward the feeling of wholeness and say, "This is what I want." Use that imagery and know that it is going to manifest in the present for you, then totally accept it as a part of you. Every day that you work with it, you are going to see more and more clearly why that was a whole time for you. You will find yourself altering life to be more like that time. You will not go back to being thirteen years old, but you will remember the kind of attitude to life and people you had then. You are going to begin to really see everything in relation to the wholeness, and then you will begin to act that way. Work with it for a week, and you will be amazed at what begins to happen in your life. In the following chapters, we will go further with this material. Remember, it is the essence of the time you felt wholeness you are reestablishing, not the incident per se.

There are no "half-packages."
You get the *whole* thing.

—Julian

The first environment
that must be changed is
you and your immediate space.
—————————————————————Julian

MANIFESTATION

CHAPTER ★ XI

Exercises in Manifestation

In working with manifestation, you will very often experience recall of negative statements casually made by yourself from before. It is important to realize that while it is not your intention that these statements have a power over you; they, nevertheless, do. Everybody does this without realizing it. They program themselves to be less. You do not realize that the casual statement is still a statement. It is still accepted by the subconscious and released through the pituitary to the body.

Visualize yourself as you want to be, but understand whatever you visualize yourself as wanting to be has a whole package that goes with it. The person who wants to be a celebrity gets all the pressure also. Do not make it a personality thing; rather, focus on a quality. See you as you want to be. That visualization can assist you.

Very often the first step toward the total manifestation may seem different from what you expect. It may be the interim step which permits you to release a hold on something or clarify your interest. I have a perfect example of this: A woman owned a boat which she no longer had an interest in owning. She received an offer to rent the boat. This was a first release from ownership. By renting the boat, she was manifesting movement toward a separation of herself from that space. It is a release of you from the boat which is the first step in the sale of the boat.

Many times, as you work with this material, you may realize that most of what you desire turns out to be trivial. What is wrong with having something trivial? There is nothing wrong with being a little frivolous once in a while. It is healthy. If there is something that is going to give you joy and is not harmful to another, there is no reason why you cannot manifest it. Maybe that will help you to realize that you can manifest other things.

As you begin to manifest, what you ask for may take a different route in coming to you. It may cause an emotional change, a mental attitude change, or it may come from somebody from whom you would least expect it. Gradually, what you are looking for will come from it. When you are asking for the manifestation, do not give directions. Do not decide whether or not it is too frivolous—unless you come up with that in the "why." The only reason we give you the "why" is so that you will take a second look and not do something that would prove to be less than beneficial for you.

Accept that what you wish to manifest will come. It will. Literally, acceptance is the key word—acceptance that it can occur, acceptance that it is occurring even now. Do not judge yourself as you go. Be willing to look at it to be sure it is a sound thing for you and that it is not something that is going to be detrimental to you. Do not ask for too large a jug of wine, so to speak, when a glass or two will do.

When working toward a manifestation, the realization that an attitude change coupled with the acceptance that you are worthy of it can put the whole thing in motion. The family gathering you used to dread can now become a pleasant occurrence. Why? Because you have first accepted your worthiness and, therefore, do not feel threatened. Secondly, you have released your old attitude and are, therefore, sending out different vibrations. This combination creates successful manifestation.

When you are putting all of your energy into the manifestation of something, there comes a point where you have to accept that it is so, which means that you do not have to continue to put energy into it. Manifestation should be as natural as saying "Good morning." It should not be a stressful, pushing, straining occurrence. By letting go with the acceptance that it will be so and going on to something else, the energy shows you that it is working.

Sometimes you will internally know when to relax with it. When you back off, it is not with a sense of failure. When you let go of it, you let go of it with the realization that it *is* happening, that it *is* in process and it *will* be.

You put the energy into it by relaxing with it and accepting it, not by becoming tense about it. It is the same thing with healing. When you heal someone, you say, "I believe in healing; it is happening." The next time you work on that person, you should be saying thank you for the healing that is in process. You say, "I continue the healing that is in progress, and thank God for it." That is what you are doing. By releasing it with acceptance, you know that it is going to happen.

In the manifestation process, you will find that there are lessons and realizations learned along the way about the self. You will know more about yourself when you are done than when you started. Realize that a manifestation has to have consideration; it cannot be a forced issue.

When you have an incident where you want to manifest something and a blockage from within says no, not now, your own high self, your own super-conscious self, can be telling you that it is not the right time. You then go ahead and prepare for when it is the right time. Work with it as if it was already yours. Recognize that this manifestation is not denied, but will better serve you at a different time. Turn your attention to another area in the life, work with this manifestation at the same time. Keep in mind that the original goal will continue at its own pace. For instance, to manifest something, you assist it by saying, "I want to manifest a business of my own. Let the manifestation come through the quality of me." See that it can still be manifesting, even while you are working on something else.

There are many other methods you can use to manifest. You may use any method you want, but if you are using fifty-seven different methods, you are not believing in any of them. You have not accepted that it can be so. You may be thinking, "Maybe I had better bring in another one—and another one—just to be on the safe side." Remember, there is nothing wrong with using them, but make sure that you are using them, not because two are better than one, or ten are better than two, but because you really believe that it is working. You must recognize that you are going to have it. If you accept totally that it is going to be there, it does not matter what method you use. You have to believe that it can be.

You do not have the right to manifest anything for another beyond happiness, security, and health. You do not have the right to say get her the blue car, or him the red one, but you can ask that the transportation problem be solved. You do not know what specific thing is right for them; you do not know what their soul growth is. If you wish happiness for others, and some specific thing is a part of that happiness, it will be manifested for them.

Do not try to dictate other people's lives. Send them joy, love and health, that which makes them able to manifest for themselves. You can affirm that the right and perfect job be theirs, but never bring manifestation for another to the point where you are making the decisions for them. Let what's right and perfect for them occur, and you do not have to worry.

Always be willing to realize you do not really know what is right for another. You only know what is right for yourself. When you work with another, you have to be willing to recognize what is right and perfect for them to manifest. Sometimes where relationships are concerned, this is not easy. You should be asking, "What can I do to better understand the relationship and let the relationship be harmonious?" Do not think that you can go in there and chisel away a new form for somebody else.

One often wants to help others, and giving to another is good, but you must also recognize that you have one energy. Instead of trying to concern yourself with their needs, why not teach your friends to manifest and then hold them in your prayers? This may sound selfish, but that is not what I am saying. As I have said before, you cannot scatter your energy and expect it to work effectively. You must focus your energies.

To manifest you have to know what you want, and the only one who can really know that is you. A person might tell you what he or she wants, but if that individual were to go through self-discovery, they may find that is not really what is wanted at all. Do not get caught in thinking that you have to make everybody else's wishes come true. Make others aware that they must make them come true for themselves.

I am trying to make it clear that manifestation calls for concentration and focus. Loving them, wishing them well, and praying for them are the only methods you should use.

It is the old story. You feed a man a fish and you feed him for one meal; you teach him how to fish and you feed him for a lifetime. No matter how hard you manifest, if they are not manifesting for themselves and making the energy effort for themselves, it is not going to happen. You may say you want them to have something until you are blue, but if they are not interested enough to do something about it, it is not going to happen. Acceptance is the key to manifestation, and you cannot accept for other people, only they can accept. Bless them, love them, and let your thought be that what is right and perfect will occur.

Sometimes people are overly influenced by what others think. If they mention that what they are working on in manifestation and someone disagrees with it, they will have a tendency to doubt their ability to bring it forth. These people might better keep their manifestation focus silent until they begin to realize it works.

Everybody has a separate body chemistry; everybody responds to different times in the day. Because of high technology, it is often stated that midnight to two a.m. is the best time for meditation, because there is not as much atmospheric interference. However, if getting up at two a.m. is causing you to be a total wreck, it is certainly not conducive to meditation. You must take that time which is right for your body. If you are going to manifest, you can manifest at any time. If you say I have to get up at two a.m. in order to manifest, you have already taken the control away from you and given it to a time zone. Know that you can work on manifestation any time and meditate at any time that is conducive to your well-being.

By concentrating so hard on what it is you wish to manifest, you are not accepting it, but are trying to force it. Do not make manifesting a stressful thing. You say, "It's going to be, this is it, it's all right," and by not thinking about it too long, you give proof that you believe it is so. In the beginning, there is a tendency for people to want to push so hard to make it happen that they are like the child holding his breath. Release yourself from that kind of tension. Take a comfortable time to concentrate and focus with it. Use the words, "I accept," and then go about your business.

The first thing you do when manifesting prosperity is look to see the prosperity you have. How is your health? Do you have a roof over your head, food in your stomach? Do you have friends? This is wealth; this is prosperity; so do not say that you do not have anything. First recognize that which you have. Once you can recognize that which you have, you can then ask for a greater abundance in any area. Negating what you have creates a blockage to more coming into your life.

There are times when the inner self understands a need that the conscious mind has not yet registered. The inner self is sending out signals for manifestation. These seem to occur unbidden in the life and are very helpful. Meanwhile, the conscious self is pushing for something else. This also manifests but does not seem permanent or fulfilling. The conscious self focuses on desire, while the inner self works on need. That is why meditation and time with the inner you is so important. That is what the question "why?" is all about. When you do want something—why? *How* important is it in the total life? Do not, in that process, allow yourself to come to a point that negates your ability to have what you want. Do not take the attitude that anything that comes is all right, because you cannot have what you really want. Instead just allow yourself time to fully relate to your inner being, then anything that comes will be right and perfect.

Passiveness and acceptance are not the same. Acceptance says, "I have the right to have it as long as it is not harmful to myself or another," whereas passiveness can say, "Well, here I am. I hope somebody sends me something." You have to be sure that you are using an action in your thought pattern.

You must realize that, while you *learn* from something that is not right for you, you do *not* accept that it is right for everything to go wrong in your life. When a pattern is repeated, a change is needed in the *individual.*

If you look at everything you would like to manifest in your life, it becomes quite obvious that some of them can sit on the shelf for a while. Manifestation of absolute need would always take priority. You should work through them first and go on from there.

When you have done your manifestation and you see signs of it coming to you, accept that it is there. It is on its way. You hold it in your mind as yours, as something you have accepted as all right, and you will find then that it strengthens that in you. Now you are free to go on to something else.

As manifestation arrives, should you feel overwhelmed by it, do nothing. Let it rest. Let it take care of finding its own path. Always remember that no decision is necessary immediately. If it is here now, it will be there later. It is right and perfect, so rest with it for a little while.

We have spoken about working with manifestation by the cleansing of the self, the letting go of the blockages of the self. No matter how advanced you become in manifestation, you should periodically give yourself a good housecleaning. Take them out and look at them—the angers, the resentments, the things you thought were so important.

There are constant references in your world to something denied in the past, and therefore, the absolutely traumatic need to have it in the present. Sometimes it is declared from seventeen lives ago and sometimes it is declared from early childhood. You have to recognize that something denied at the age of five, or whatever early age, cannot have a power in your life at the age of twenty, thirty, or forty, unless *you* have given power to it. You are not five, six, or seven now. People *choose* to hold onto a thing that was traumatic at some early age, forgetting that they are no longer that age. As you let go of the angers and resentments, understand that you are releasing things that do not really relate to the present. When you are releasing, be sure that you really release. Do not dig it up and chew on it again. Look at it from the present age, the present comprehension, then let it go. You will find a much greater release is yours.

The American Indian has a statement about walking a mile in the other fellow's moccasins before making a judgment. When you go back to a "he said," "she said," "we said," "they said" sort of incident, try putting yourself in another person's shoes. You would be amazed how different the situation looks. To the five-year-old who wants a cookie, it is the most important thing in the world. To the mother who just looked at the dentist bill, no cookie is the most important thing in the world. It is a matter of timing, age, focus, and viewpoint.

In manifesting, it is important to recognize that a single manifestation can affect the entire life. When I say the entire life, I mean every level of the life. If you are talking about the manifestation of something, you are talking about your emotions, your mental attitude and your physical self. Whatever you manifest will affect *all* of you. If you are looking to manifest a relationship, that relationship is going to affect the mind, the body, the emotions; it is going to affect how you interact with other people; it is going to affect the very atmosphere that surrounds you. That is why we ask the question "Why?" when we manifest. "Why? Why do I need it? Why do I want it? Do I want it out of anger? Do I want it because I have been denied it at some point and, therefore, I must have it now? Or do I want it in the form that is right and perfect for me?"

Many people create false reasons why they want something. If I were to have a penny for every time I have heard in your world, "I want to win the lottery so I can do good for people," I could fill a room. Everyone of those statements would partially be a falsehood. They do not think it is nice to want it for themselves. Honesty says, "I'd like to win the lottery so that I can have the life-style I want, which includes helping other people." Then, why do you want to help other people? Is it that you need to say you did this so you can be proud, or can you give it without anyone knowing you gave it? When you give without anyone knowing you gave it, you have truly given. The emotions, the ego level, all of you are affected by everything that you try to manifest in the life. You must be ready to really look at what it is you are asking for, because when you get it, you are going to have to cope with everything that goes with it. You will receive the whole package. Do not be afraid to really ask "why?" Once you feel that you clearly know why you have a need for this in your life and if it is a healthy thing for you, then manifest it.

Visualization is very important in manifestation. It is not easy to visualize a companion. If you are saying, "Five-foot-two, eyes-of-blue" and some charming tall redhead walks in, you are in trouble. You have limited who may come to you. Suppose you were to see a figure that responded to you walking in a door. Visualize every incident in your life where you could see acceptance of you. Remember the time when you ran into someone's arms and were totally accepted? Maybe you were five years old at the time, but the joy of the incident is there. What does relationship mean? Trust? Gentleness? You have to know what you want in quality and envision the atmosphere which that quality creates.

If you want someone who is generous and gift-giving, think of all the times you were given gifts; think of receiving. If you want to mother, think of all the times you have mothered. Think of the atmosphere, the emotions that went with that which you are trying to manifest. If it is peace and harmony you want in your life, think of the times that have been peaceful. Let the atmosphere of that time actually be absorbed by you until, when you think of what you want to manifest, you feel it. You feel the exuberance of the joy of a relationship, or the absolute peace of opening a bill and knowing that the money is there to pay it. Think of every time you have paid a bill and felt good about it. Every time a bill comes in, let that energy surround you so that the next bill will also be paid. You create the essence of what it is you want, and you let that manifest for you. You think of that which represents what you wish to manifest, but not with a forceful attitude. You think back in your life to the times when you felt very good about yourself, the times when you felt very constructive, when you felt *you* were in control.

The person who is afraid of speaking in front of

groups must remember the times of self-confidence, so that the confidence to do this can be reinstated in them. If you are afraid to be in front of a crowd, you may find it hard to look back and see yourself in front of a crowd confidently. You look back at other times when you did feel confident and then you physically go about making yourself confident. In other words, if you wish to manifest getting up in front of a crowd to speak, you know that you must have the confidence to do it. You think of all the times when you felt in control, and you let the energy of that time surround you. Think of all the times you were in control. It might not have anything to do with speaking in front of anyone. Then make sure you know your subject. That is your physical contribution to it.

If you let your mind go back to those confident times before you get up to speak, you will speak without fear. You will manifest that confidence, because it is not speaking in front of people that you are trying to manifest, it is confidence. It is the ability to be in control of yourself. That is why you search out the real reasoning behind the manifestation, so that you understand what it is that you are really trying to manifest. You have to go back and think of times when it happened, when you felt good about yourself, when you felt all together. You must permit yourself to really feel that you have the whole thing. In other words, you are feeling it, not just saying it.

To a person who cannot visualize easily, snip a picture out of a magazine, put it in a folder and look at it periodically. If confidence is what you are trying to build, find a picture that depicts somebody in charge, somebody in control. Put that picture in your folder and look at it daily and think, "That's me; I can do that." In this way, you have a visualization that you can touch. Understand that manifestation is a technique of using your own self-confidence to bring the things you want into the life.

The same confidence can be directed outward to larger issues. The use of positive thought directed with confidence can bring great change. There are many situations in your world which are not to the greatest liking. Therefore, you should picture your world in a happy situation. Literally, take your earth, as you understand it, and see it as if it were smiling. See it surrounded by the brightest, most beautiful colors that you think would be proper. Heal it. Lay your hands on it if necessary, but know that you accept totally that it can be so. If you only see the evil, you are not helping to change the evil. You have to see that it can be so, and if you yourself are living as a person who is giving, then you are already changing the energy in the universal bank. If you are feeding your children properly, or helping in some way to nourish yourself, you are putting nourishment and food in the universal bank. That is a better use of your energy than worrying about it. Worry is a negative energy that adds to the negativity. Accept that it *can* change, and do what you can physically to make the image of change real.

EXERCISE I

I would like you to be quiet and take several deep breaths, breathing in peace and harmony and breathing out all anxiety. Breathe in peace and harmony, and breathe out all anxiety; breathe in peace and harmony, breathe out all anxiety.

> Now think of that which you wish to manifest. Hold it in your mind.
>
> Ask yourself: "Do I feel the same about it as I did last week?"

Tell yourself: "If I do feel the same, let me intensify the feeling of it."

"If I do not feel the same, why? What is different?"

If something is different, reshape and focus that which you wish to manifest now.

If it is the same, continue to intensify the comprehension of it.

Now ask yourself what emotion it evokes in you.

How does it make you feel?

Is it beginning to function more strongly within you?

I want you to begin to feel as if it were here right now. You can reach out and drive it, you can hug it, you can wear it. You can live it, feel it, know it.

Accept totally that it is yours and that you deserve it.

Say to yourself: "I accept."

Now release it.

Take a deep breath and let yourself be aware.

When you use this method, you are "putting your money where your mouth is." You are not just talking about it, you are being still with yourself about it. You are taking it internally and beginning to express the real association with it. As you work with it your feeling when you concentrate on it becomes stronger by giving it more impetus to be. It is beginning to work and function with you.

Sometimes you will receive from the higher self, from the super-conscious self, input into what you are trying to manifest. It might be something you have to look at in that manifestation, or it might be something that is saying this is not so good for you. Ask to understand it fully. If you find no relationship to it, then cease manifestation for that period and go back to it another time. If the same things keep occurring, then it definitely has a relationship which you must begin to track down. When you understand the connection, you will have a clearer manifestation goal.

When you think of any situation, it is far easier to remember the irritants of it than it is to remember the joys. For instance, you may have a long ride to see someone you love, but when you come back, you think that that was a long ride. You forget the joy of being there and the joy of visiting, but it does not mean you did not thoroughly enjoy it. Anything that is an irritant to the self has the ability to get your attention. When you look at the qualities of yourself, very often you have a tendency to do the same thing, to look at the negatives or irritants of yourself.

In learning to recognize your value, the first thing you begin to do is think of the things you have done that are good. What are the things about you that are right? What are the things about you that are worthy? What are the joys in your life? As you remember and think of those things, begin to see that there is a lot that is very good and worthy about you, and they may very well outweigh those things that you think of as negative.

Remember, we are talking about qualities here. We are not talking about whether you are too short or too tall, too fat or too thin. Those are physically oriented attributes. We are talking about you in terms of your real self and about seeing the qualities in you. Recognize that, for most of your life, you have been attuned to a reward system. The good boy gets the cookie. You feel the need to perform to get the reward.

Within man is the feeling that, unless he does something outstanding, he cannot deserve anything. If you work at trying to be a good person, if you support yourself to the best of your ability, if you are trying to understand the higher part of yourself, then you are doing what is right for you. That effort should be recognized as worthy.

There is a tendency to look at what others are doing and feel you should be doing that too, or to feel that you cannot possibly have something because somebody else does not have it. That kind of energy put out into the world helps to "have not." If you are always saying you cannot have, you are putting "have not" in the universal consciousness, which eventually will affect the universe. Know you have the right to have, and from that, you are putting into the universal consciousness the ability to have.

Look at the things you do for other people and recognize those qualities in yourself. If there is a failing that bothers you a great deal, then do something about it. Start changing things. If you have been evasive with yourself and others, start being direct. If you have been afraid to voice an opinion, voice an opinion. Take that which you see as a weakness and begin to work on strengthening it in its *positive* sense. The next time you take a look at yourself, you will not feel so insecure, because you have taken steps to rectify that which bothered you.

Every time you feel like putting yourself down, change the thought. Accept yourself. If I could, I would put in three-foot high letters for all to see a most important word—*accept*. Accept yourself the way you are. From that point, by the acceptance, you are able to change it. You are not fighting it; you are joining it and working with it instead of against it. Remember you cannot change anything until you have accepted it in its present state. From there you can begin to see and act upon the necessary changes.

Humbleness is acceptance; humbleness is not subservience. It is accepting that where you are is all right, and you can, by that acceptance, change it. It is not fighting the environment, but joining it in acceptance. *It is all right for things not to be all right*. The moment you accept that, you take its power away. It is only while you are fighting it that it is an irritant that can negate you. The moment you recognize that the incident is the world of appearance and that the world of reality is within you, you have the ability to shape and form your reality. You then are able to work with it. Accept you as you are, and know that you have the power to change what you wish to change about yourself.

EXERCISE II

I would like to start this exercise with an affirmation. We are going to go through a series of statements. The first is:

God is, I am, and we are one.
I am His divine being.
I release all anxiety.
I recognize my worthiness.
Thank you, Father, that this is so.

Quietly repeat those phrases to yourself.

Now visualize that which you wish to manifest. Feel its essence. Feel it moving closer to you. Accept that it is yours. Sense it, feel it, as if it were here right now. Now repeat these phrases:

> I am free.
> I am worthy.
> I accept.
> So be it.

Release yourself.

EXERCISE III

Please close your eyes and repeat:

> I am a divine child of God with divine rights of my own.
> I shall manifest them through my self to the benefit of myself and mankind.
> I accept it.
> So be it.

Please use this. Let it grow, let it build. Every time you work with it, it will grow stronger and more powerful until you see God acting through you.

Freedom is not doing as you please, but being pleased with what you do.

———————————Julian

**When the dance of ego
ends, teamwork begins.**

—————————————————————Julian

CHAPTER ★ XII

Centering Toward Manifestation

When the first thrust of manifestation occurs, the energies begin a conversion. They come together, and it appears that everything is happening just the way you want it. There is an automatic relaxation inside yourself. This relaxation is the indication that you have really accepted the process. The energies then seem to become nebulous again until a redirection of the focus occurs.

When it seems to be going wrong, there, is a tendency to fall back and feel it is not working. It is like going into a new endeavor of any kind. At first the excitement is so strong that you think, "Oh, this is the greatest," and, after a while, you think, "I'm not so sure," because other things begin to have an influence on it. Do not give up. Stay with the focusing and manifesting. Sometimes a disruption will occur in manifestation when the timing is not right. Do not let the world of appearance and its negativity let you stray from directing positive input.

When you are directing the energies toward health, anything that disrupts that manifestation will have a short life. You may, find yourself not feeling "up to snuff." This will last only a short time, because the power of the health manifestation is stronger *by focus* than the nebulous release of the various irritants in the body.

If a career is the direction you want to manifest, ask for what is right and perfect for you in the career avenue. Before you direct manifestation energy to an individual career, it is best to think about various careers. In the process of thinking about them you will identify more strongly with a specific one. In the process of thinking about them, you bring in an ability to focus on a specific career. Now ask to be shown which one is most compatible to your energies. This will be the one that is right and perfect for you to work on manifesting.

When you think about a career, do not decide that you are going to be a prima ballerina when you have never made any effort to learn dance. That is not focus; that is a fantasy. The man who wants to be a runner is first going to learn to walk and then to run. He is not going to wake up in the morning a prime runner. There is a logical physical sequence that goes to manifestation, and you must work with that as well.

When you are trying to manifest a new direction in your life, you have to be willing to let go of the old. There are times when something changes in your life and you find that the things you were relying on are no longer there. Now you must accept that there is something new in store. It is really a commitment of your faith to that which you really want to do. Very often, this process may seem as if it is going into reverse, and that is why I say do not let the world of appearance deter you from believing that it will be.

Whenever you are creating a change in yourself, you are reshaping or reforming yourself to a degree. There will be residue that will come to the surface that you have had within you for years. You may find that there are parts of yourself that you do not like, or that even shock you. All of this is the housecleaning, the coming to grips with the fact that you have faced a part of yourself. You do something for one reason, when all the while, lurking behind that reason, is something else. Those nooks and crannies will empty out, and you will get a clear look at your reasons for doing things. That is a revelation that is sometimes a shocker, and when that occurs, it can be a traumatic sort of thing. It is a purging, a letting out, a cleaning house, which gets rid of things that do not fit. It is a healthy and productive process.

If you have not liked yourself for a long time, and for the first time you are permitting yourself to like you, it can be a tearful reunion. Tears are not always negative. They are a manifestation of inner emotional release. They are the self in expression. Enjoy your tears and enjoy getting to like yourself.

At times when working with manifestation, you may feel isolated or deeply removed from the reality of yourself, almost as if you were "on hold." Do not worry. God is not on hold. Blessed is he who waits. Know with a certainty that, because there is truly a time for all things, the waiting can be the adjustment to the proper time. It is important to have that time. Know that God is not on hold at all. You may be on hold, but not God. That is all part of the focusing and the directing. You do have to spend time with yourself, and sometimes it can seem like a long wait.

There is often the tendency to want to help another overcome some difficulty or affliction. You cannot interfere with something that one must experience. You may want to manifest the man next door getting rid of his stereo, but if he has a right to the stereo, it is going to stay. It does not mean you have failed at manifestation; it means that you are trying to manifest that which is not in your control. Instead, try manifesting your ability to block out the sound or his choosing to lower the volume.

When manifestation of health reaches a certain point, know that there are certain things that have to go with it. If you try to heal a body too fast, and a cell has not had a chance to go through its proper levels of strength and orientation, it could cause problems later. There is timing involved in healing; there is soul growth involved in healing; there is karma involved in healing. You have to manifest what is right and proper for the individual receiving the healing. When a person is afflicted with an illness, you have no understanding of why he is experiencing it. You do not know the whole story. Your manifestation can only help to give him courage to go through whatever he must experience.

You cannot interfere with someone's karma. You cannot interfere with something that must be. The healing energy you direct to them will be converted to the courage, patience, and tolerance that they need to withstand whatever it is that they must go through. Healing is never lost or wasted, nor will it interfere with a karmic pattern or soul growth. It can only help it.

The first step in your self-development is to accept yourself. The moment you accept yourself, you can change anything you want to change in you. While you are beating yourself down, you do not have the strength to change anything. Remember, to be humble is to accept yourself. The moment you do that, you can make any change in yourself you want. Know that, as you are able to love yourself, you are able to be loved. Nobody can be loved if they do not love themselves—and that is not ego. It is acceptance.

As you work with the manifestation energies, you will occasionally come upon blockages. You will feel as if it is not working, and then the little demon that says, "Can I really have it? Do I have the right to it? Am I worthy of it?," comes creeping in. You begin to have a feeling of unreality where your manifestation is concerned. It may be that you need to re-evaluate why you want to manifest it.

When you are manifesting something, it may be right and perfect for you at that moment of your life, but three months later, there may be something else that is right and perfect in your life. If you try to manifest the same thing, at that time you might not find it comfortable. Once you are adept at using manifestation energies, you will be able to know instantly when there is something not quite right, when the gears are not quite meshing. By backtracking on attitudes and reasons, you will probably locate the blockage.

If you are trying to manifest something in your life that you would not know how to handle, or which would do you more harm than good, you may have blockages occur. It does not mean you cannot have it eventually, but you have to look at why you are trying to manifest it. Question whether you are ready for it.

Many people say, "If I win the lottery, then all my troubles will be over, and all my friends' troubles will be over." First of all, that is the thought that says, "See, I'm worthy. I can have it because I've got all these good thoughts about what I'm going to do with it." In reality, winning that lottery can create a lot of friction in the life. It can create a lot of misunderstanding. People need people. People have interaction with people in their lives for various reasons. If something occurs in the life that puts them in the position of thinking they do not need anyone, it can be one of the most devastating, unhappy experiences of their life. It can be a very dangerous thing and a blockage to soul growth. When there is a time of winning in the life, it will occur only when the life is *inwardly* in balance. Then it will manifest. Recognize that it will be held in abeyance until it is right and perfect in your life. It is also a test of your belief. Anyone can have faith when things are going well. How many have faith when things are going badly?

Saying "I am God" is quite different from saying "God and I are one, and *together* we can do all things." There is a difference between an ego-ridden manifestation and the acceptance of the partnership. You will know when it is ego-ridden because it will have no consideration for anyone else. It will be *me, me, me, me;* but it will never be me in relationship to others.

Within you is the full potential of the Father. He created you in His image—not one head, two arms and two legs, but in His energy. He created you in the image of full potential. The creative force dwells within *you*. When you get in touch with it, you are in touch with the God within you, and *you* will manifest those things in the manner that is proper for all concerned. There is no ego involved, only the willingness to manifest Him in the physical world.

God does not "lay it on you," as you say. You have to manifest him through your physical act in the world. The dancer must practice, the typist must practice, the pianist must practice. God gives them the potential and the talent; the individual makes the decision to be a pianist, a dancer, or a typist. They must practice and use the energy to make it manifest. It is a working partnership between the energies of the physical plane and the energies of the highest plane.

Anything you do with love and in joy is an expression of God. Every time you complain when you "must" scrub a floor, or wash a dish, you are denying God. For in every act and in everything on earth, He exists. When you wash a dish or scrub a floor, that too is in the image of God as well. It is not a case of separation—this list is of God and that list is not. Raise any incident to its highest energy and it is He. You are His vehicles in this world. Therefore, you must put your mind and energy to the manifestation of His will. He has given you the raw clay, now you must make your sculpture.

You have to take off old shoes before you can put on new ones. That is common sense. It is the same with anything you deal with, whether it be emotions or material things. You have to stop hating something in order to love it. It works. It is always there functioning, but it is a power that you have to use. This power is given to you by the Father. You may use it, but you must know that you are using it as His *partner* and are, therefore, using it for the good of yourself and mankind. The moment the ego steps in, you have broken the contract. You may still manifest, but it is going to be rocky. Remember that what you manifest comes back to you. You have the whole package and you must handle it.

The concentration in manifesting has to be an acceptance, not a forcing. Do not let your concentration become a forced issue, but rather let it be in the form of a relaxed acceptance.

If you have an inner desire that is in direct competition to what you are trying to manifest, it is going to keep coming up and blocking it. It is when you are at ease with the situation that by acceptance, the greatest energy works, not when you are trying to hammer it home.

If you have never looked at life from the space of being fine, but have always looked at it as a struggle, have always looked at it as having to get help, you will need to change your attitude. Watch those thoughts that block your own manifestation. It is like building the blocks up and then kicking the bottom one out; you have to start all over again. How you see the situation you are in at the moment tells you how you are looking at life. Often when things do start to go right, panic can set in. How do you handle it? How do you handle having it *right?* For so long you have struggled with what was wrong, it is difficult to know how to react to things going right.

You may find yourself busy with life's activities and not able to sit and formally work on manifesting something. Deep within you, however, the desire is there. That thought pattern is working because it is a heartfelt thing. Those thoughts continue working even in sleep state because they are not superficial but deep-seated.

Manifestation is a power. What you direct energy toward will manifest, but there are no half-packages. An ego-ridden manifestation will have to have the backwash of an ego, and therefore, you will have to come to grips with it. You will know when your thoughts are ego-ridden because they will have no consideration for anyone else. It will be *me, me, me.*

The universal laws work. Manifestation has nothing to do with where you are coming from in terms of a belief system; it does not have anything to do with a dogmatic practice. A non-partial energy is brought into power through the process of focusing. As long as you can focus your thoughts in relationship to what you are trying to manifest, you can make it happen. Just remember, the universal law says you get the whole package. Thus, it behooves you to think through the full ramifications of what you are trying to manifest before you start.

You do not have to spend your whole life doing focusing exercises. If you have developed a clear, concise picture of what it is you want to manifest, you have it. All you have to do is think of that picture being there. You do not have to force it. The focusing is to know *what* you want and *why* you want it; or, at least, why you think you want it. From that focus comes all else; from that, other things can begin to manifest.

There are times when a sleep state is a healing process. It is also a natural instinct used to get away from other pressures. The body, the mind, and emotions run to sleep as an escape route from pressure of any kind. If there is a great energy being put out and you are feeling fatigue, the body is going to signal *time out* and sleep. If the need to sleep stems from poor nutrition, you must begin the process of changing your eating habits. This type of sleep alone would not be able to revitalize the body. As long as you can say you are not trying to run away from anything but you are tired, sleep is fine.

We are going to try to work a little bit with the realization that within yourself there are physical, mental and emotional blocks. Each of these affect your manifestation. I will put this on a very material level as an example.

Suppose, as a child, you were very chubby, and you always wanted a red dress with ruffles. Suppose you were always told "Chubby children do not wear red dresses with ruffles." There is a mental image building of yourself as a chubby child. Secondly, there is a mental image building of red dresses with ruffles being "forbidden fruit." Thirty-two years later, as a size nine, you see a lovely red, ruffled dress. When you see the dress, you not only experience the pleasure of it and the joy it gives you, but immediately there arises mental memory that it is forbidden fruit. Logic may say it does not make any difference anymore, because you are no longer the chubby child. You are now in a position to wear this dress very attractively, but the mental block is there. You will not really feel comfortable with red ruffles until you release the old pattern from the subconscious and reprogram it.

You have to examine why you are feeling the blockage. You need to ask yourself when was the first time you felt that the dress was a forbidden thing, something that was not for you. When you find that point, go back with it further and begin to find out what your emotional relationship was to that mental block. How did you feel when you were denied it the first time? There is often a tie between that first denial and how you may feel if you get it now. You may overcome the mental block and say, "I don't care whether I'm supposed to have it or not, I'm going to have it!" Go to the mental blockage, identify the emotion you felt when it was first there and, from that point of origin, start changing the blockage by letting it be released to *that* point in time. Eight years old—chubby—red dress denied—terrible rejection and unhappiness. Why? Not only because you could not have the dress, but for the first time, you realized you were chubby. For the first time, you realized there was something "wrong" with you in the eyes of other people.

When you find that there is something uncomfortable with a manifestation point for you, go back in time to where it is mentally stuck. As you think about it, you will succeed in recapturing that point in time. You have had it pushed down in you so long that the moment you really start looking for it, it is going to pop up. The difference will be that you are not going to be looking at it as an eight-year-old, chubby child; you are going to be looking at it as an adult with a comprehension of who you are. Through this process, you can experience the release and enjoy life without doubts or guilt.

EXERCISE

Think about that which you wish to manifest. Now say:

I accept it; it is mine.

Think about it and feel where it seems uneasy to you, where you feel there is an irritant, or a discomfort. Now say:

Here is the blockage; I search for the emotional point.

You are going to sit quietly and think about it until you remember the emotion associated with the blockage.

Now, you may get a little teary; do not let that bother you. It is just a release and it is all right. As you release it, you are going to think of the age you were when it first happened, and your statement at that point will be:

I place it in that point in time.

And then:

**I free myself and release it
to that point.**

If the same kind of rejection happened at several points in your life, you go back to the first one, because the first one is the one which made you susceptible to the rest. You are searching out the point in time when it first occurred. You are then going to free yourself by releasing it to *that* point in time.

This exercise is only used if you find yourself uneasy or blocked while trying to manifest something. This is done when you find yourself uneasy, when you find yourself blocked. You must find out why you think that way and what emotion is attached to that thinking pattern. Let it go back to the point in time and the age you were when it first happened. Now recognize that point in time at age so-and-so. If you do not know the exact age, name one close to it and release the blockages to it.

Take a deep breath and make yourself comfortable.

Think about that which you wish to manifest and make your statement:

I accept it; it is mine.

As you think of it, let it become quite clear in your mind and then ask yourself if you feel uneasy about it at any point. If you do not, go right on focusing.

When you have found a point that is irritating, go to the mental point (how you thought about it then).

And now the emotional point (what feelings were evoked).

Now release it to that point in time. Free yourself. Take a deep breath and repeat:

I am free. I rejoice.
I am happy. I am fulfilled.
I thank God.

Now, come back.

When you release to a point in time, you forgive everybody involved, releasing them to that point as well. You recognize that what occurs to you at one point need not be carried through your entire life. Every time it starts to well up again, re-release it until you really get it out. Say, "I release this to its point in time. I bless it and let it go. I am free; I am happy; I am joyous."

You can attach to something early in life which can become a real stumbling block mentally and emotionally later. Until you go on a tracking expedition and find it, you may think it is related to something else. You may find that some of the people you were attached to were those whom others made you feel uncomfortable about. Somehow you felt you should not like them. Aunt So-and-So may not have been the pillar of society, but she was fun. You can remember the adults saying, "You know Aunt So-and-So," with *that* tone. Later, when you meet someone who has the attributes of Aunt So-and-So and who is fun, you may feel uncomfortable when you are with them.

There are so many ways that you are subtly influenced from the past. It is *not* always somebody doing something to you, but rather how *you viewed* a situation. One of the best experiments you can do is to put yourself in the emotional and physical positions of someone else. For one day, or one hour, go around with a blindfold. Get down on your hands and knees and see what the world looks like to a two-year-old, and you will understand why some things frighten them. Can you imagine what it looks like when a group of six-foot people look down at you if you are a child? The child must certainly feel that there is some huge thing about to attack it.

Sometimes when you go back to the thinking pattern and emotion, you will realize they do not go together. There is a third emotion. For example: You remember the first time you felt naughty. Somebody had died. You didn't understand death and you were caught giggling at a time when the rest of the household was solemn. It is not the death that emotionally ties you to that moment, it is the sense of guilt. There was an attitude expected of you which you were not able to deliver because you did not understand it. There are mixed emotions, and they need to be understood. When you find that dual energy, search for the real cause of why the guilt is there.

Early in the life, attitudes may be developed that become handicaps later in life. The desire to be different may be born out of a need earlier in life and then used later in life as a tool. For instance, in business relationships with superiors, you may refuse to recognize their authority and later have problems all born from some adolescent experience which has long since passed and is today of no importance in the life. There can be such an imprint developed of the need to flout discipline that you will flout disciplines that could be very constructive to you later in life. At that point, those attitudes are not serving you well.

When you have difficulty releasing an emotional point from earlier years, think back to when you were at that young age. Ask yourself if you are *now* two years old. You can hold on to a viewpoint of a two-year-old, or you can look back to other incidents that may have happened at that age and recognize that that is where the emotion belongs.

Have you ever heard how parents talk to their children, "The boogeyman's going to get you!" "I'm going to give you to the policemen; they're going to come and take you away." The power to release traumas from those early experiences is in you. Do not judge the actions of your parents. You view them with today's mind and understanding. *Remember that repetitious statements determine whether you hold or release something. Watch your statements.* The subconscious has held those memories in its little nooks and crannies. Therefore, you need to release it regularly until the subconscious feels you really mean it.

Take time out to be silent with yourself, to permit yourself to release all those little "thorns and nits." Let them out knowing that in the release, you are giving yourself a new lease on life.

It is human nature to hold on to attitudes, even when you don't like them. "It may be a bad habit, but it is mine, and I'm not going to give it up." The repetition of a statement is needed to assure your subconscious that you *are* going to give it up.

Whenever you go into this exercise, tell yourself, "I'm going into it joyously with a wonderful opportunity to release negatives that are bothering me and making my life heavy." Do not approach it with, "I must give it up." That statement says you do not want to give it up. Anything that says you are not in control of the situation creates opposition energy. If you are told that you cannot go down that hall, the only thing you want to do is go down that hall. You want to find out why you cannot go down there.

When you work with this, do it with joy, know that you are letting go. Use visualization that you can feel and see. Think of something that is a negative for you, for example, standing out on a hot July day with fourteen sweaters on. Visualize every sweater coming off, one by one, and with it, a part of the negativity going away. You are going to feel so relieved to get all those sweaters off on a hot July day, and with it will come a release from the negativity. When you use a visualization, make it pertinent and make it powerful. The visualization makes it easier and easier for you to rid yourself of the things that make you unhappy.

When you start working with release of negative blockages within, it is better to attack one issue at a time. When you feel it is truly released, try another. This is better than holding up a bushel basket of attitudes you feel may need to be changed. After all, how on earth are you going to trace them all down at the same time? How are you going to know which emotion is associated with which event? Single out one. What you are doing is opening yourself up so you can go down the long dark corridor with a flashlight to find the light switch which puts the lights on for the whole corridor. You are saying, I am taking a point in time which is a mental focus point. By going down the corridor to find what emotion is tied to it, you will find the light switch and give yourself light. By doing that, you are bringing everybody else light as well. Every time you feel the emotion, you remind yourself that it belongs in that other point in time. You let it go; you bless it; and it is gone.

The control and focus which make things happen in your life are already yours. One cannot be passive about their life. There is a working partnership between divine will and yourself. When you say, "Thy will, not mine," it does not mean sitting passively and waiting for Him to make up your mind. It means having the courage to take the divine gift of free will that He gives you and make a decision and work with it. Be willing to accept that there are times when you may make a mistake, but even a mistake would be a soul growth experience and to your benefit. To trust that you can make a decision is the first step. "If God is with me, then all things I do will be to my benefit. I will make the decision that is right. His will, His faith are mine." It is having the trust to trust that puts it all together for you.

When you are working with manifesting and have done all in your power to make it occur, and it does not seem to be getting results, then accept that there is a power beyond you that is holding it in abeyance until its right time. God did not give you all your abilities to waste. He gave them to you to use. You do make decisions in life, and you will fulfill yourself through those decisions. Recognize that if it is a decision that is not to your best advantage, you have still learned from it. In that sense, it has not failed you. This is the reason for asking yourself "Why?" What is the real reason you want it?

**Believing is the power
that makes wishing a reality.**
—Julian

**Beautiful pottery
starts out as mud;
a little shaping
makes the difference.**

——————————Julian

CHAPTER ★ XIII

On The Way

This chapter will discuss group manifestation. Just as individuals are able to manifest, so too is it possible for groups or countries to manifest. There is no end to how much collective energy can be brought together for manifestation, but in that collective energy, there has to be a focus. If I were to suggest to a group that fish is nourishing food and simply ask them to concentrate on their favorite fish, there would probably be diverse thoughts, each according to individual tastes. Energy might be directed to cod, flounder, or pickerel. There would be multiple fish-thoughts. Therefore, when a group wants to manifest, it has to focus, and have an absolute understanding about what it is they are trying to manifest. They must totally understand every aspect of it, and they must go through the same cleansing attitude that a single individual would go through in releasing energies of anger and resentment.

Always remember that you can not bring *good* into your life while you are thinking and wishing *no good* for another. There are no half-packages. It is a case of *clean up the whole act* or *do not try*, and so it is with a group. That is why a group will not understand why the success they have been looking for has not come. It is because they have not truly focused in one place and sent the energy to that place. In other words, a collective energy must be a single energy when it is manifesting.

This can be helpful to you, because one is always involved in groups of some kind. It can be any kind of group. It can be a group of office workers looking for improvement in their office. It can be collectively bringing help to someone. It is any sort of collective endeavor brought to a single point of energy and manifested as such. You can all do it, either singularly or collectively.

The one thing that creates a manifestation process for you in a very strong pattern is your belief. Just as you cannot love when you hate the man next door, neither can you manifest when you do not really believe it can happen. Your lack of belief has negated the manifestation. By believing that it can rightfully be yours, that it is yours, and already is in your possession, you only have to rediscover it in you. You are then able to work with it.

Know that you will manifest that which is right for you. You cannot manifest something wrong for another and have right manifestation for yourself. Do not think about using manifestation energy to harm another, because if you do, the only place the harm will come to rest is in you. Everything you send out is like a boomerang. It is naturally going to come home to roost.

We have been talking about manifestation energy as if it were a separate entity, but actually, it is a part of everything you do in life. It is a part of how you believe; it is a part of how you act; it is a part of how you go about your work. In other words, when you are manifesting something in your life, it is not just at the time you sit down and do a manifestation exercise. It is how much you believe in it the rest of the time, how much you let the rest of your life truly reflect it. That is why the person who claims to be spiritual cannot simply sit in a *spiritual* group and say they are *spiritual*. When they go out the door, it must go with them, and they must interact with other people in a spiritual manner.

When you are truly ready to accept and try to change your life, you may feel afraid. You may feel yourself saying "Show me the way," on one hand, and wanting to run from the answer on the other. If you feel dissatisfied with yourself, you very often expect that whatever you are shown will be a judgment of you.

The moment you begin the process of being willing to see the changes, they will begin to manifest in many ways. Not only will paths to investigate be shown, but doors will open. Things will happen. What you thought was so hard before will suddenly seem easy. Things will begin to change. You will let it happen by the realization that it can, that it will, and that it is all right.

It is not selfish to manifest in the life; it is taking your partnership with the Father seriously. If you think God will do it for you, good or bad, or that it is all His fault, you have "copped out." It means that you take no responsibility at all for what you do. Live the principles of the Father, and from that, you will form a partnership which permits you to assist *Him* in manifesting in *your* life. Remember to take a moment to say *thank you* when it arrives. Show that you know and care that it arrived, for that makes all the difference in the world.

When you first choose to manifest, very often the thing you choose to manifest is not really what you need. It is what you *think* you need. As you begin to see or feel the energies move, you have second thoughts. You take another look and you reevaluate it.

Because the dream is one of the most advantageous ways of getting messages to you from what is stored in the subconscious, you very often will have lessons in the dream state. I have a very good example of how this works. A student from one of my classes went through considerable frustration in his early stages of learning manifestation. He had started using these techniques and, shortly thereafter, began to have a number of fears about his manifestation. In the practice of working with the manifestation energies, he even modified what he was seeking, but to no avail. He felt very strange all the while. The process climaxed with a nightmare in which he operated on someone's brain and literally removed it from the head. He woke up petrified. He realized it was his brain, and he was being told he had short-circuited it. He was not ready to come to grips with the focus of his manifestation energy, and he short-circuited it. For him, this in itself was a tremendous realization. If you remember that the brain is a mechanism for the thinking process, you will recognize that in operating on the mind, you are altering what comes to you, for as a man thinks, so shall he have it brought unto him. He needed to look at where he was directing his manifestation energy and find out why he felt the need to short-circuit it.

There is no conflict to manifesting something in your life with "Thy will, not mine." If you are trying to manifest proper health, you may meet someone who can treat you by holistic methods; you may meet the surgeon who is proper for what needs to be corrected. "Thy will" will bring the means to health, but the health manifestation has to have your stirring of the energy to attract that to you. You recognize that there may be more than one way that it may come to you, and the best way for it to come to you will be what manifests for you. If your manifestation were in direct conflict to karmic patterns, it would not manifest, so "Thy will, not mine."

You need to understand that when the Father created,

He created the energy method for the perpetuum (perpetuation) of that which He created. The metaphysical energies that can be used were of His creation for the perpetuum of man's understanding of the higher part of himself. Every master teacher who has come to this earth has said the same thing—that man, through love, through God, through the centering of God, will do that which the teacher does.

At first, you may take off thinking, "This is it; I know exactly what I want! Oh boy! Here we go!" Halfway through, you begin to say, "Wait a minute. What have I got by the tail here?" It is the tiger-by-the-tail sort of thing, because there is more manifesting than just "a thing." The manifestation of soul growth is occurring, and consciousness levels are changing. The entire pattern of what you are manifesting is affecting you on every level of your life, not just on a material plane.

Sometimes when you have found the origin point of the blockage and there is difficulty in releasing, it is because you have attached other points to it. It is like a cobweb with many, many threads that go out in many directions to many points in time and to many places in your energy pattern. Until you trace it like a thread to its point of origin, you cannot really let it go. Try to see what other things are feeding it. "I can't let go of this sadness—why? What is there about it that makes me want to be sad and stay sad?" If you do not let go of that sadness, it can become the vessel for all sadness.

There is a part of man which feels that he does not dare be totally happy, because if he is, someone is going to come along and take it away from him. That is tied to some form of feeling unworthy in the past. Trace back what has come and attached itself to the feeling. Go back to the first time you experienced the feeling; then go to the next time you felt it. For instance, you felt sad because there was a death in the family. Your grandmother died. You were only three years old when the death occurred, so you did not know grandmother very well, and you did not understand death at all, but there was a pall of sadness over the house. Therefore, when death is mentioned, sadness comes, even though you do not understand it.

When you are ten years old, your dog dies. You loved that little dog. Now there is an understanding of something being taken away with that word "death." The sadness now has a pain with it, so the second experience renewed the first feeling, but also brought an understanding with it. From that point, you may go to another death experience and, perhaps, find out that there are compounded circumstances. Your brother's wife dies; you never really liked her. There is guilt. There is not only sadness because you are supposed to be sad at death, and pain because you are supposed to have it, but now there is guilt about it. All along, death has been built up in your mind by these collective experiences. Go through and find the other barnacles that have been attached to the original vessel. When you cannot quite let go of something, you have to go back to the origin point, discover what caused them, and release them.

Another thing to realize is that, if you have impregnated the subconscious with a particular feeling, it takes repetition of the opposite feeling to release it. You have to give it time. If repetition does not release it, do a tracing to see what other energies have begun to feed the original energy. Only then will you release from it.

If you tie yourself to a point in time emotionally, you cannot move forward in the present. When you look at an incident from your present understanding, you examine it with the understanding of *now*. You can now see that reaction and energy from the previous point in time and are now able to release it.

Very often, when there is an emotional expectation within yourself, you build in an escape route. It can be a statement that says, "I'll do it for so long, but I won't be able to maintain it." Already you have negated your ability to maintain it by that statement. You must start feeding yourself a new statement to remove that old attitude. If you cannot trace it, it is something you are working with in the present, as well. Tell yourself that you can sustain anything in your life as long as you want to.

There is an expectation prevalent in your world of falling apart at the age of sixty-five. Everybody has to be retired at that time; the mind cannot function anymore; everything goes wrong. Of course it goes wrong! Your culture programs this into you from your childhood. Poor old grandpa! "Old"—"poor"—bad news! The closer you get to grandpa's age, the more you are convinced the body is going to do exactly what grandpa's did. No. You are whole; you are healthy; you are well until your last breath—whenever that occurs. Do not accept that you have to follow a demise of the self because of some strange programming in the culture. Methuselah (a Biblical patriarch who lived 969 years) was no accident. He lived beyond the years of most men. You manifest every moment of your waking hours. You are constantly manifesting, even when you are not consciously thinking about it, so be careful what you think—you might just get it.

The person who says, "You know me; I'm always late," is manifesting lateness in his life every time he makes the statement. People who do this are accepting that they are always late and then wonder why they are not invited to interact with others. They do not connect their statement to what is happening in the life.

I can remember, not too long ago, looking at the world and hearing people say that Europe was so far away from your continent, and it is now a matter of hours away. Americans think nothing of going to Europe today. It is a constantly changing world. What you thought of as an absolute at one point in time is not an absolute at another, so you have to be willing to look periodically at what you are programming for yourself.

A child who has been told often enough not to climb a tree, later in life, will probably have a hard time climbing a tree until he tells himself he can. He must change the thought pattern that is there, because underneath, he is constantly programming himself. Listen to what you say in casual conversation. Play a game called "Pull-The-Rug-Out-From-Under-Me-Every-Time-I-Hear-Myself-Make-That-Negative-Statement." Say to yourself, "Wrong! This is the truth for me now," and affirm the opposite.

As a child, you do not determine what you are going to accept; you are still in a programming situation. You have parental influence, teacher influence and peer-group pressures. Because you have not solidified a thinking pattern of your own, you are accepting everybody else's. As an adult, you come into control of what you are going to permit to become a part of you. That does not mean that you will not be in negative situations, but you do not have to accept them as your own. If somebody says, "I don't think you are able to do that," you reply, "I think I can, and I'd like to give it a try." You do not say, "I guess I probably can't; you're right."

When you are in a situation where there is negativity, do not join the negativity by saying everybody is so negative. "I can't do a thing because everyone's so negative." No. You say, "I am in a positive spot; I am a positive point," and as long as you are, you can handle it no matter what goes on around you of a negative nature. It is only when you join it without thinking that it begins to have a real power over you. Think a moment when you are in a negative situation to prevent yourself from joining it. Instead, permit yourself to go forward from a positive point.

Tracing back to origin hurts does not mean you do not feel the pain, but you can let it begin to dissolve. By realizing that today's circumstances are different from then, you have everything necessary to make it different. By changing your perception of the incident, it is easier to let it go.

It is important not to spread yourself too thin. You have to really know where you want the energy to go. Remember you have one energy, and you can only focus that one energy in one place.

The way to know whether you should manifest or not is to ask yourself if you are happy. If you say no, you have to make changes and manifest differently in the life. If you can say yes, you are content and happy, you probably have already manifested many fine and wonderful things with which you are, at that time, content.

If you say you are happy and someone asks you if you believe that, what do you say? "Well, maybe not." Then you did not believe it in the first place. If you say, "Yes, I do," and they ask, "How can you be?," you say, "Because I am happy—are you?" If you are happy and content with your life, you have been manifesting that which *your* life needs, and you have it all.

Remember that the techniques of manifestation are to help you understand that you can work with them and control them. It is not meant to be a checklist—this week the house, next week the car, the next week the fellow. No. It is to help you see that you can manifest change through the use of the powers that God gave you. You can change your life.

There is a tie between your physical senses and your spirit senses. In the meditative state, you create the harmonic between them. That harmonic opens the door to the universal consciousness. It is like having the right frequency. Patience is always very necessary, and it does seem that it is the hardest thing for mankind to learn. Know that as you are willing to give it the discipline, understanding will occur. Practice in your physical world the art of seeing and hearing. Really listen to what is being said; really see what is going on.

You respond to any moment in your life with the consciousness and emotional understanding of the moment. That does not make it wrong; it means that it is your response at that moment. The next moment, a week later, a month later, or ten years later, you will still be looking at it, but with a new consciousness, one which says that it was not the best decision—but not wrong. Do not judge.

Above all, love yourself unconditionally and know that when you are working with manifestation, it does stir things up. I am not teaching you to go out and ask for anything you want; I am teaching you to know why you want it. I am asking you to examine your values and know in your heart that it is right for you. That stirs up all sorts of hornets' nests, but by looking at them, you relieve yourself of them and life is smoother.

Look at the other person and see the God in him. "The God in me sees the God in you." In other words, instead of going around in a negating way, go around in a positive, constructive way that says, "I see the good in you, for if I am seeing it, it must increase. It must be there to bloom. If I am only seeing the negative in you, I'm helping that to bloom." To love one another unconditionally means to love, not by a checklist, not by a performance rating, but because God is, you are and You are one, and so are they.

To love one another unconditionally is not to judge. If you start judging that person, you join them. You have become exactly like them. See the point of God in that person. That is what you love and bless in them. No one can hurt your feelings unless you let them; no one can make you angry except yourself. Those are your responses to the energy. Therefore, when you are dealing with someone who appears to be negative, do not join the negativity. You have the divine right of discernment, which says that you do not have to accept that as yours.

Does it matter that somebody has done something wrong to himself? A person takes drugs. It is detrimental to their body. It may not be right for you, so you do not accept it for yourself, but you do not damn them or you are joining them. Judgment belongs to the universal law of cause and effect. It is always in motion. It is always there; it is always working. Nothing is ever gotten away with, so man does not have to worry about that.

When someone hurts your feelings, ask yourself why your feelings are so easily hurt. Maybe what they are saying is true, and you do not want to listen. Maybe what they are saying is not true, but you do not know how to say it is not. Sometimes someone will say something, and you are stymied. You know it is not true, but you do not know how to explain, so the chance to make the correction is gone. You are stuck with not having opened your mouth. This happens to many people.

The point to remember is this: People will act negatively in the life—by whose standard? The people who want to take drugs, take drugs. They will tell you they can stop at any time, that it is not detrimental to them. By their standard, it is fine. Your response is to say "by whose standard?" You do *not* make anything a part of you that *you* do not feel is right for *you*, but do not judge the other fellow. You love him unconditionally on a spiritual level. Loving him unconditionally does not mean taking him into your bosom, into your home, and becoming one with him. It means to love the God in him. I do not have to be one with him, nor do I judge him. That is the little nuance that is different.

A challenge that is soul growth always has a workable ingredient; a negativity will always have a direct attachment to a negative action given. A person who has always been short-tempered, who has never seen the good in anyone, who has never been able to give of himself, will have a lonely life. Loneliness is a negativity for that person, but it has been attracted by what he has handed out—pushing people away. There is always a direct tie to the negativity that is visible. You can actually see a correlation.

The challenge will be something that gives you an opportunity to work in a productive manner toward an end. If one has an invalid parent to take care of, it may give the appearance of blocking your life. In reality, it may be delaying some of the things you would like to do at that point and time, but it is not denying those things to you; for later, there will be the opportunity to enjoy. In the interim, the soul will have grown from all the work that has been done, provided it is done in a loving manner. If it is done with hate, you will not have attracted to you the good, or the fulfillment, at a later date.

It is normal to feel a partial resentment to anything that confines you. You love your children dearly, but there are times when you think that if you did not have them, you would be free to do what you want. It is a momentary thought and does not mean that it is your real feeling about the children. It is a momentary mood, or thought, that passes. You realize that and say, "So much for that. I really want them; I love them; and I know I will do whatever I can for them." You have already answered to that; you have erased it. However, if with everything you do, you tell a child, "All this is because of you. I've done without because of you. My life has been miserable because of you," that child is not going to be much help to you in your old age—and neither will anyone else.

Sometimes when you change an old habit, you are not quite ready to take on a new one. A perfect example is if, immediately following a divorce, one jumps into another marriage. You have not had time to find yourself as an individual. The moment you know yourself, you can go into another union without comparisons to previous associations. It is like giving yourself time to breathe. It seems unpleasant because you feel alone and need love, but it is a time that gives you a sense of freedom and understanding that permits the next union to be happy. What seems negative is the preparation which permits the polarity to the first experience to occur.

You must also realize that there are times when you must remove yourself from an energy. I have heard people say, "Every time I go there, it's the same thing, they end up in a fight." If it upsets you so much, why are you still going there? You have to be willing to change where you go. Alcoholics should not hang out in bars. There is no way they are going to avoid being tempted if they do.

When you know there is a negative atmosphere, do not go there. Tell yourself that it is ridiculous to put yourself in this position. Remove yourself from the atmosphere of negativity. Look within to see if you are creating it in yourself, and seek to change those attitudes in you. When you learn to handle it, you will go. It is really a decision of common sense.

Understand that every place is impregnated with the energies of those who are there. The atmosphere of a room after people leave has everyone of their energies impregnated in it, and the atmosphere in that room will feel different from their having been there. A chair that you always sit in has your energy in it, and another person sitting in that chair may feel your energy. A bar has a certain type of energy piled up in it. That energy is the atmosphere of that place. We are not saying it is good or bad, but it is there, and what you feel when you go in is whatever has been experienced there. Because it is a place, many times, for release of unhappiness and loneliness, unhappiness and loneliness may be lying there. You not only leave your footprints in the sand, but in the atmospheric factors of every place you go.

EXERCISE

Think about that which you most want to manifest in your life and think of it in relationship to its effect on other people.

How will it affect other people?
How will it affect you?

If the answers have been pleasant to you, you know that you are in safe territory. If it has not been harmful to another or yourself, you are free to manifest it. If you have felt, at any point, that it is harmful to another or yourself, then do a trace on what you felt:

"Why do I feel it is harmful?"

"What is my relationship to why it is harmful?"

"What is it I fear from it?"

Think for a moment what it would be like if this were already in your life.

How would it change your life if it were already there?

How would you change your life?

And now, I want you to bless it and let it go, knowing that it is there to manifest, if you choose, at another time.

EXERCISE FOR GROUP MANIFESTATION

This is a method for a group manifestation. I ask that you manifest peace. I want you to think of a symbol that you think of as peace in your world. On a universal level, the dove is very often thought of as peace.

I want you to see your symbol of peace enter your heart. Feel it as a Light symbol entering your heart, filling you. You are peace; you are full of peace.

Now, I want you to picture your world. Picture the globe, as you call it, and see that globe surrounded by misty Light, sparkling with heavenly bodies.

And now, see, coming from your heart, the symbol of peace you have chosen. I want you to see it wrapping that globe and celestial surroundings in absolute love. You, from your heart to the world, are sending love, peace, and harmony. I want you to picture that until the entire globe is also Light which radiates from the globe through the constellations. Know that your heart and those radiations are one. Accept it now. Peace be with you. Peace fill you. Peace surround you.

The following phrase is given phonetically. Chant it aloud and hear it within you.

YO WAY AH. YO WAY AH. YO WAY AH. YO WAY AH.

The phrase means: The God in me, the love in me, is given to you. It is universal love expressed through sound. Do you feel it? Do you feel the power of it? It is the sharing of the heart and the soul. It is the giving. When you are feeling down, look at yourself in the mirror. "Yo way ah." Give it to yourself and know that Light and peace and love become yours. Know with a certainty that this sound can take you out of any depression you are in, but you must look yourself in the eye in the mirror so that you speak to your soul.

Behold the children of the universe vibrating in peace and harmony—at one, at one, at one. My blessings are with you. Thank you for permitting me to share.

Julian

The dance of the day is sunlight;
the song of the night is moonlight,
dance and sing, and become a star!
———————————————————————————————Julian

JULIAN TAPES ★ ★ ★ ★ ★ ★ ★ ★ ★ ★ ★ ★ ★ ★ ★

#105 UNIVERSAL LOVE
#201 HISTORY OF THE UNIVERSE (4 TAPES)
#202 DREAM SYMBOLISM & INTERPRETATION (4 TAPES)
#203 JESUS THE MAN—MYTH & REALITY (4 TAPES)
#204 SPIRITUALITY IN EVERYDAY LIFE (3 TAPES)
#205 ATLANTIS & LEMURIA (4 TAPES)
#208 EGYPTIAN INITIATIONS (4 TAPES)
#209 UNIVERSAL LOVE (4 TAPES)
#210 SELF-DISCOVERY (4 TAPES)
#211 MANIFESTATION (4 TAPES)
#212 HERMETIC LAW #1 MENTALISM
#213 HERMETIC LAW #2 CORRESPONDENCE
#214 HERMETIC LAW #3 VIBRATION
#215 HERMETIC LAW #4 POLARITY
#216 HERMETIC LAW #5 RHYTHM
#217 HERMETIC LAW #6 CAUSE & EFFECT
#218 HERMETIC LAW #7 GENDER
#219 PREPARATION FOR SELF-RELIANCE (2 TAPES)
#220 DECISION MAKING IN THE NEW AGE
#221 FAILURE: THE GREATEST SUCCESS
#222 SENSUALITY AND SEX
#223 YOU ARE UNIQUE
#224 THE GNOSTIC GOSPELS (2 TAPES)
#225 INTRODUCTION TO REVELATIONS
#225c KEY TO REVELATIONS (2 TAPES)
#226 MANTRA MAGIC
#227 MONEY MANAGEMENT IN THE NEW AGE
#228 MODIFICATION OF DISEASE
#230 DRUID & ESSENCE CULTURES
#231 UNIVERSAL ENERGIES OF NUMBERS
#238 HANDLING INFIRMITY IN YOURSELF AND OTHERS
#239 THE RUNE STONES (2 TAPES)
#240 THE RAINBOW EXPERIENCE
#241 RELATIONSHIPS (2 TAPES)
#242 HEALING TOOLS AND THEIR USES
#243 HERBAL ALTERNATIVES
#244 UNIVERSAL ASTROLOGY (2 TAPES)
#245 A NEW AGE INTERPRETATION OF THE ANCIENT RUNES
#246 HUNA (2 TAPES)

★ ★

#247 THE ART OF HEARING
#248 THE NORMALCY OF REJECTION
#249 THE ELEMENTALS
#250 UNDERSTANDING AND CONTROLLING ANGER (2 TAPES)
#251 NUTRITION FOR BALANCE
#252 THE DRUIDS AND THEIR TEACHINGS
#253 MEDITATIONS TOWARD ACCEPTANCE
#254 REINCARNATION
#255 SELF-ESTEEM (2 TAPES)
#256 POWER, FORCE, & SPIRIT
#257 CEREMONIAL MAGIC
#258 CONTROLLING ANGER PHASES III & IV (2 TAPES)
#259 JULIAN'S WORLD
#260 THE ANIMAL KINGDOM
#261 SOUL SEALS (2 TAPES)
#262 WRITING WITH SPIRIT
#263 SPACE CIVILIZATIONS
#264 THE ROOT RACES OF MAN
#265 TUNING IN & TUNING OUT
#266 THE BOOK OF REVELATIONS (2 TAPES)
#268 WRITING WITH SPIRIT PART II
#269 GETTING IT TOGETHER
#270 TAROT-THE MINOR ARCANA (2 TAPES)
#271 KYOS AND NUTRITION (2 TAPES)
#272 THE POWER OF PRAYER (2 TAPES)
#273 ENERGY TRANSMISSION
#274 THE SPIRALS OF EVOLUTION & HOW THEY WORK
#275 LIVING IN THE MOMENT
#276 CREATING YOUR OWN ROAD MAP FOR THE NEW AGE
#277 BELIEF GRIDS
#278 THE THREAD BETWEEN ALL METAPHYSICAL PATHS
#279 THE PARABLES OF THE MASTER TEACHER JESUS IN TODAY'S WORLD

For further information about these and other tapes of Julian and June Burke, send your request for a descriptive brochure and price list to:

Rev. June K. Burke Enterprises
Route 3, Box 133
La Grangeville, NY 12540

Personal Notes